TEATIME
IN THE
NORTHWEST

**THE NORTHWEST'S BEST TEA ROOMS AND
RECIPES FOR TASTY TEA TIME TREATS.**

Sharon & Ken
Foster-Lewis

SPEED GRAPHICS
SEATTLE, WASHINGTON

About the authors

Ken and Sharon Foster-Lewis live on a quiet corner of Camano Island in Washington State.

Ken hails from Liverpool, England where his life experience was as varied as jumping out of airplanes with the British Parachute Regiment and working as a dancehall bouncer during The Beatles' early days. He has also lived in New Zealand.

Sharon grew up on the Oregon Coast and met Ken in 1978 in Alaska where she was working for the airline on which he was a passenger.

A shared love of nature and world travel carried them to numerous international ports of call before settling in the home Ken built for them overlooking the tea-time sunset on the sparkling waters of Puget Sound.

Acknowledgments

Front cover photograph © 1996 by **Chuck Hill**

Special thanks to **The Perennial Tea Room** for providing the classic teapot used in the front cover photograph.

Special thanks to **Kamian J. Dowd** for providing teapots from her collection for use on the back cover.

Photograph of Sharon and Ken Foster-Lewis on the back cover © 1996 **Unlimited Exposure**, Stanwood, WA (360) 629-6383

Printed in the United States of America.
ISBN 0-9617699-6-3

Dedicated to the memory of Ken's father
Hughie Lewis
who gave us our first tea set.

TABLE
OF CONTENTS

INTRODUCTION

I admit it now. Years ago, when my English mother-in-law, Emily Bell Lewis, entered the guest room I had carefully decorated for her first visit, looked around, and pronounced it "homely," I may have been at a loss for words. And when Emily was rummaging hopefully through my cupboard looking for tea and came upon a teabag, which she dangled in front of her face for a moment, I really think now that it was my rich imagination and new bride insecurity that made me think she was eyeing it as though it were a dead mouse.

I soon learned, to my relief, that "homely" meant cozy, warm, and comfortable to an Englishwoman. I also learned there is a whole world of tea to be explored and enjoyed.

It was a year or two later, when Ken and I were on a hike through the foothills of the Himalayas in Nepal that I really began to think of tea as more than a simple beverage. We were honored to be invited into a private home near our trail. Through our bi-lingual Sherpa guide, Sonam, we learned that we were invited to share tea, chai, with the household. We had no shared language with which to converse, and yet the sense of companionship and graciousness experienced over that chipped porcelain cup of tea with yak butter bridged our two cultures. Nothing else embodies the true essence of hospitality like sharing tea. While sitting on a simple bench set by the open fire of that mud-floored dwelling, I learned that tea is by nature "homely."

A Brief History of Tea

All the tea in China

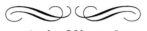

*. . . At the fifth cup I am
purified;
The sixth cup calls me
to the realms of the
immortals.*
　　Lu T'ung

Like the thick fogs that often shroud our Pacific Northwest coastline, so too has the origin of tea been clouded through time by myth and legend.

Scholars seem to agree that in the year 2,737 BC. there existed an enlightened Chinese emperor, Shen Nung, on whose silk-clad shoulders rest at least one of the accepted versions of the origin of tea. Shen Nung was revered as "The Divine Cultivator" and "The Divine Healer" and was a person whose advanced knowledge of hygiene predisposed him to boil his drinking water. One day while working in his garden, several glossy, green leaves with serrated edges drifted into his cauldron of hot water. Glancing up, he noted that it came from a tree bearing a lovely pure white flower. Shen Nung discovered as he bent over his cauldron that a delicate and pleasant aroma was emitted as the water gently boiled, and so he filled a ladle and tasted it. Now thoroughly pleased with the recuperative properties of this tasty, refreshing brew he immediately issued instructions to his subjects to carefully cultivate the plant, today known as Camellia sinensis, a distant cousin of those harbingers of spring gardening, our camellia bushes.

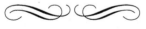

*Drink tea that your
mind may be lively
and clear.*
　　Wang Yu Cheng
　　Sung Dynasty

India and Japan also lay claim to the discovery of tea, and it is safe to say that the plant was growing in those areas too as it is native to semitropical and tropical climates as well as in the rarefied air above 5,000 feet. If left untrimmed, the plant grows to treelike proportions of 40 feet and more and lives 70 years. It did not take early cultivators long to see the advantage for harvesting if kept trimmed to a bush of 3 or 4 feet. By 350 AD a thriving tea cultivation society had emerged.

By the 5th century AD tea had become as popular a trade commodity as vinegar, rice, and noodles, making its way along established trade routes to Persia by sure-footed caravan. The subtle shift had begun from considering tea as a medicinal and natureopathic substance to a pleasurable social beverage and major bartering tool.

By 780 AD, enterprising tea merchants sought a forum to promote their product. In commissioning Lu Yu to create the masterpiece essay Ch'a Ching or The Classic of Tea they had found a means to put forth detailed instructions that served to unify the cultivation, preparation, and enjoyment of tea. Until its publication, information on all aspects of tea had been passed on orally. The book had far-reaching effects, some of which were not anticipated by the tea merchants. Government revenue officials, tirelessly on the trail of ways to augment their coffers, levied the first tea tax. It is an excellent indication of how deeply ingrained tea had become to the culture that the unified cry of outrage by the tea-drinking populace was actually heeded by the officials who rescinded the tax for 13 years.

Lu Yu was an orphan found wandering by a Buddhist monk. Not at all enamored of the austerity surrounding his adopted father's calling, Lu Yu did what young boys have wanted to do for centuries; he ran away and joined a circus as an acrobatic clown. While performing in the provinces he shared his ebullient energy and talents with countless people, one of whom became a benefactor. Through this mentor Lu Yu was introduced to books and provided with an education. So it was that Lu Yu, orphan and clown, became a scholar, author, cultural celebrity and friend to an emperor before retiring to the life of a mountain hermit where he died in peaceful introspection in the year 804.

So poetic and detailed are the instructions set forth in Lu Yu's essay that they have survived for more than 1,200 years and today form a basis for the beautiful ritualized Japanese Tea Ceremonies, "Cha-no-yu". It has been said that the beauty and simplicity described in Lu Yu's tea ceremony captured the very essence of the religious thought of the day.

We shape clay into a pot, but it is the emptiness inside that holds whatever we want.
Tao-te Ching

"The cup that cheers" - Tea and Europeans

We had a kettle; we let it leak.
Our not repairing it made it worse.
We haven't had any tea for a week . . .
The bottom is out of the Universe.

    Rudyard Kipling

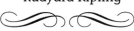

At about the time that Juan de Fuca's ship was plying the waters of Puget Sound in search of the elusive Northwest Passage, sailing ships bearing Portuguese Jesuit priests were riding anchor in the bustling harbors of China. One of these Portuguese ships had been navigated by a Dutchman with a literary bent, Jan Hugo van Lin-Schooten, who in 1595 published a journal of his travels and described in glowing prose the wonders of the Orient, including tea. The journal captured the Dutch imagination and they wasted no time at all in establishing a trading base in Java to which more than 60 round-trip trading voyages would be made in the first seven years.

By 1610 the first Chinese teas were shipped to Europe by the Dutch. By the mid-1600s, tea had been introduced to Britain, France, Germany, Holland, Scandinavia, Russia and America. The Germans and French were quick to shrug off the new beverage, returning instead to the comfortable familiarity of their ales and wines. The other countries adopted tea as a beverage of daily consumption, but in England tea virtually entered the national bloodstream and was embraced with the same passion they held for the playwright of the day, William Shakespeare.

Revered in Britain as a cure-all and health elixir, tea was restricted to the aristocracy and kept under lock and key for its first 50 years there due to its high price. Tea was first offered to the public in London in 1657 at an Exchange Alley coffee house and tobacco shop owned by Thomas Garway. A handbill (or "broadside" as they were called) passed out by Garway to promote sales imbued tea with medicinal and moral powers of almost magical proportions. Reminiscent of later day TV "infomercials", the virtues attributed to tea were "boosted memory, cured fever, rid colic, eased brain, and strengthened stomach muscles".

The Dutch held what amounted to a monopoly on trading tea for some time, but after a combination of bloodshed, upheaval, and diplomacy, The

British East India Trading Company grasped control of much of the tea trade from the Dutch. By 1700 tea was being imported directly to England on its own ships, and so the prices dropped. More than 500 coffee houses in London were then able to offer tea as well. Eager horticulturists even tried to grow the evergreen tea plants in England, but found no cooperation from the climate there to do so. Nonetheless, tea had finally made the transition from being the exclusive nectar of emperors, tsars, and kings, to the daily table of the common man.

Tea, Toil, and Trouble in the Colonies

Late in the 1700s British tea merchants commissioned American shipbuilders to develop and build a class of sailing ship designed specifically for the tea trade. The clippers, as they were called, were three-masted, graceful and fast. Capable of transporting one million pounds of tea each trip, their speed dramatically reduced the voyage time. Fortunes were now being made and lost not only in the commerce of tea but also in gambling on the outcome of the annual 88 to 102 day duration race from the harbor in Canton around the Cape of Good Hope past the Azores and into the English Channel. Finally the clipper ships were towed up the Thames and the precious cargo rushed to waiting London auction houses.

The celebrated tea clipper Cutty Sark

There are few hours in life more agreeable than the hour dedicated to the ceremony known as afternoon tea.
    Henry James,
    Portrait of a Lady

Meanwhile on the other side of the Atlantic, dissatisfaction was growing in the colonies at the same rate as the taxes being levied upon them. While many British taxes on goods bound for America had been repealed, the three pence per pound of tea stayed intact. The relationship between America and England would not. In 1773 American colonial housewives united under the name "Mistresses of Families." In what amounted to a boycott, this powerful consumer group vowed to rid tea from their tables until the rapidly increasing taxes were repealed. It was also suspected that England was keeping the best tea for themselves and sending inferior product to the colonies. The colonial womens' scandalous "uprising" set tongues wagging in the gentile parlors of London tea parties, and planted seeds for an even larger uprising in three years that would lead to the loss of the colonies.

The high taxation and shortsightedness of the English government was not limited to the colonies, however. In England the duties added to the tea by the government had raised the cost for a pound of tea to four times the average man's weekly wage, and the taxes levied on tea reached 120%, with much of the revenue earmarked to save the financially beleaguered and generally mismanaged British East India Company.

*And freedom's teacup
still o'erflows
With ever-fresh
libations,
To cheat of slumber all
her foes
and cheer the wakening
nations!*
Oliver Wendell
Holmes
*Ballad of the Boston
Tea Party*

Smuggled Goods

High duty and high demand for tea combined to make smuggling a lucrative vocation in England. The intricate coves and hidden inlets that make the southern England coastline so charming were the perfect setting for the clandestine off-loading of tea. Small vessels plied the moonlit waters to meet the large commerce ships, most of them Dutch, silently riding the swell offshore. The lucrative business of tea courier caused a farm labor shortage in the south of England as a network of swift and strong young men conducted the business of transporting tea to shore by small boats and then on to secret caches as diverse as church crypts and castles throughout the countryside. At one point, 50% of the tea off-loaded to English shores was contraband. Most of the able-bodied young smugglers that were lucky enough to be caught alive by the revenue officials were conscripted into the navy.

Meanwhile in the colonies, another group of able-bodied young men under the name of "The Sons of Liberty" were determined to make a more dramatic and visible statement against tea taxation. On December 16, 1773, disguised as American Indians, they swarmed onto ships off-loading tea and dumped 340 large chests of tea into Boston Harbor. The British Parliament was swift in meting out punishment by enacting strict laws designed to penalize the rebellious colonists and to limit their political freedom. In the colonies the cauldrons of revolution simmered and bubbled like the tea kettle, and the First Continental Congress convened. The country mobilized for its fight for independence. Tea had started a revolution.

Finally by 1784 the tax on tea in England was reduced to 12.5% and the benefits that had been derived from smuggling were effectively negated. By now, it was far too late to repair the damaged relationship with the colonies that had broken away to form an independent nation.

The American coastal explorer, Captain Gray, had developed in the meantime a lucrative trade with our Pacific Coast Indian tribes to obtain the lush pelts of otter, mink, and beaver. These furry denizens of our Northern waters became the valuable link that allowed trade directly with the Chinese for tea. The doors to trade in the Orient swung open for the young country and tea began being imported directly to North America on its own ships.

The Duchess of Bedford's Stomach Growls

Afternoon tea began as an English institution in 1840 when Anna, the 7th Duchess of Bedford's stomach began to growl. The Duchess, a society trend setter who apparently could not get by on the two big meals a day, took to having tea and a snack of sandwiches and cakes served around four or five in the afternoon. Legions of closet-snackers looking for an afternoon lift followed the trend setting duchess and the custom spread throughout the country. The tea time was adopted by manual workers and farmers in the form of "high tea," a more substantial meal that often included meats and cheeses and more robust fare. This was often the laborers' main meal of the day.

In 1848, in what amounts to early industrial espionage, an English gentleman with the providential name of Fortune disguised himself in the garb of a Chinese merchant. Carried in a curtained

The term "high tea" came about because it was often served at the dining table (or high table) as opposed to a "low tea" (which later became known as "afternoon tea") served on a lower tea table in the parlor or by the fire.

sedan-chair under cover of darkness, and sleeping in monasteries, Robert Fortune surreptitiously garnered tea cultivation knowledge, soil samples, and processing methods in areas of China that were off-limits to foreigners. His acquired knowledge unlocked the secrets to tea and enabled the British to establish large tea plantations, known as "gardens" that thrive to this day throughout India.

Queen Victoria herself declared tea to be the national beverage of England, and she even outfitted her vacation retreat with a small scale table and plush chairs with the names of each of her children embroidered on the back so they too could participate in afternoon tea. Other teatime indulgences emerged in the general marketplace. Pottery makers sensed the demand and began competing with each other for novel teapot designs that were both utilitarian and ornamental. Suddenly merchants' shelves were awash with teatime paraphernalia.

In 1864, an enterprising manager of A.B.C.-Aerated Bread Company in London encouraged her employer to allow her to open a tea room in some unused space. It was her intention to serve tea and refreshments in the afternoon. Business thrived. Society's approval of tea had thus created the first public place where a proper lady could actually go unchaperoned. While they still would not win the right to vote for another 40 years, tea drinking ladies were heady with this new found freedom. Tea rooms blossomed everywhere.

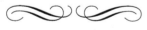

Tea . . . the cup that cheers but not inebriate.
William Cowper

Tea Rooms of the Pacific Northwest

Today, those initial endeavors have engendered a harvest of public tea rooms in Oregon, Washington, and British Columbia. As varied as the inhabitants of this beautiful area, the tea room roster in this book will have a special place to delight every reader. From the ivy-mantled, hushed tone, tinkle of silver on porcelain tea rooms to the fun, eclectic and funky tea rooms, the Northwest has a special place for you to linger over "the cup that cheers."

Lu Yu Explains Tea

Imagine, if you will, that Lu Yu is given one day back on 20th century earth and he must spend it in the Pacific Northwest. Closing his eyes and randomly dialing numbers in a phone booth, he calls your home. It's Saturday morning, you have some free time, so you arrange to pick him up since he doesn't drive.

Lu Yu is easy to spot near the phone booth in the colorful silk brocade jacket which he has gathered around him to ward off the misty Northwest chill. As he shifts from foot to foot to stay warm, you note with concern the small splash his sandals make in the puddle. "The first stop will be Eddie Bauer and Nike," you ruminate thoughtfully, "then a good cup of tea to set things right." (Fortunately, you had the presence of mind this morning to bring along your copy of TeaTime in the Northwest.) "An 8th century tea philosopher should enjoy a good 'cuppa'."

The shelves of the cheery tearoom are a feast for the eyes! The colorful tins and shiny boxes glisten in the morning light with colors to rival the richness of Lu Yu's silk jacket, (which you feel a little guilty thinking would look good with your black slacks). After apologizing for the weather on the drive over, you realize that with the topic of tea you've struck a pleasant chord for conversation.

"So many teas . . ." his eyes caress the crowded shelves with delight, lingering over the myriad of green teas like one recognizing an old friend. He makes his choice, and the pot is delivered to your table. With his waterproof Eddie Bauer jacket draped casually over the back of his chair, and the aromatic beverage creating a mystic aura over your table, Lu Yu once again takes on the mantle of an 8th century tea philosopher. As you make a mental note to remove the price tags and extra button packet hanging from his new jacket, he begins:

"All teas come from the leaves of one bush, the Camellia sinensis. It is in the processing of the tea leaves that the three different teas are created." His new Nikes squeak on the floor under the table and appear to startle him.

Tea tempers the spirit and harmonizes the mind, dispels lassitude and relieves fatigue; awakens thought and prevents drowsiness.
Lu Yu

*The goodness is a
decision for the mouth
to make.*
    Lu Yu
    The Classic of Tea

"Three different teas? There must be thousands," you assert, perhaps a little too strongly. You may not be a tea philosopher, but you do know your retail tea merchants' shelves. "Perhaps Lu Yu is a little out of touch with what's happened in the last 12 centuries," you decide to yourself.

"Three teas," he patiently restates, his voice underlining the importance of this very basic piece of tea information, "black tea, green tea, and oolong. It is the processing that determines their differences. There are dozens of varieties of each of these three, usually named for the region in which they are grown, and then literally thousands of different tea blends."

"What is this 'process' that the tea leaf undergoes?" you query, realizing this person really does know his tea.

Lu Yu inhales the aroma of the tea. He fumbles a moment with the handle on the cup, decides to simply avoid it, and holds it gently in his two hands like one would a small bird. The warmth is a welcome comfort to his cold palms. "The process is either three or fourfold depending on the type of tea. First, withering removes as much moisture as possible from the leaves. Then they are rolled or manipulated to partially rupture the leaf tissue. This step releases naturally-occuring enzymes that begin the process of fermentation. It is the degree of fermentation that determines which of the three tea types you are producing. That is what distinguishes them from each other," he says matter-of-factly.

Suddenly you flash back to a wine appreciation class you took from a local wine expert. "Fermentation?" you ponder, "Like in the production of a good wine?"

"No," he says simply and patiently like speaking to a child. "Like in the production of a good tea. The term fermentation actually is a slightly misleading technical term for the process of oxidation - the exposure of the leaves and the released enzymes to air. Finally, they are dried or fired, which stops the fermentation process and dries the leaves evenly." "Naturally" he adds, "there are numerous variations on this general process depending on the source of the leaves and also the country in which the final tea is manufactured. Darjeeling, Keemun, Assam and Ceylon are all black teas for example. Black teas are subjected to all four of the steps, Oolongs are lightly withered and rolled and only partially fermented before being dried."

"And your favorite, the green tea?" you probe.

"Ah, green tea," he rolls his eyes skyward in remembered delight, "green tea is not fermented at all. The leaves are steamed or heated rather than withered, then rolled and dried. The leaves remain green because they do not oxidize. A green tea is light and clear with a delicate, very flavorful taste." He smiles and nods toward the pot between us, "But I must say I am enjoying this black tea! As I say in my book, 'the goodness is a decision for the mouth to make'. You have read my book, haven't you?"

Avoiding his stare over the rim of his cup you assure him that it was your fond intention to read the whole book, and one day soon you certainly would, that you had been a bit busy lately. You are relieved to notice that this seems to satisfy Lu Yu.

" What a delightful experience it has been for me to see how far tea has come in 1,200 years." he actually smacks his lips after tipping his cup for the last taste and rises. "But now I really must be getting back. Do you have any other questions for me before I go?"

"Well, I read somewhere that you actually were an acrobatic clown in a travelling circus in China. Is this true?" You had been longing to ask that question all through the morning but did not want to seem impertinent nor to interupt the wondrous flow of tea knowledge. Slipping the embroidered silk jacket from his shoulders, he folds it gently, caressing the fine brocade, and hands it to you with a slight bow saying "Please accept this humble gift as appreciation of your kind hospitality," and with a smile, Lu Yu executes two perfect backflips out the door of the tearoom and disappears into the Pacific Northwest mist.

I am in no way interested in immortality, but only in the taste of tea.
Lu T'ung

The first European teacups evolved from Oriental tea bowls and were without a handle. To avoid burned fingers, Europeans poured a sip of tea into the saucer to cool. A single handle was added to the cup in the mid-18th century.

Types of Teas

My Aunt Marwayne knows the night sky. With unbridled delight she will rock back on her heels, throw her gray head back, and enthuse, "Oh look, there's Venus in Taurus! Ah, Jupiter's moving through Gemini." From the sky she can tell the seasons of the year. From the sky she can tell the seasons of a person's life. The night sky in her company seems a friendly place, populated by stars with which you are on a first name basis. I admire that wealth of knowledge and the comfort of that familiarity.

Before I got to know much about tea I had a general feeling it must all be pretty much like the teabag variety. My expectations were minimal, and the brew I made met these limited expectations nicely. It would be brownish. It would burn my tongue if I wasn't careful. It was okay. The idea of subtle varietal differences in tea had not entered my thoughts.

The following varieties of the three main types of tea (Black, Oolong, and Green) are provided simply as a starting point for your own exploration. Within these varieties are literally thousands of variations based on country of origin and even the blending techniques of various tea companies. Experimentation will help you find your personal favorites, and even to create your very own blends:

Black Teas

Assam - from northeast India, this is a robust and hearty tea with a strong malty flavor and rusty color, grown at low altitude, and used in Irish Breakfast Tea. Good served with milk.

Ceylon - from Sri Lanka, golden color, a strong full taste and delicate fragrance. Good served throughout the day.

Darjeeling - makes an excellent after-dinner tea, rich in flavor, with a flowery bouquet. This tea is grown high in the foothills of the Himalayas of north India, and is an expensive tea.

Earl Grey - a 19th century British statesman the Second Earl Grey, was given this recipe in appreciation from the Chinese for his diplomatic work. Typically drunk in the afternoon, Earl Grey has a pungent, flowery fragrance and delicacy owing to Oil of Bergamot sprayed on the tea.

English Breakfast - often either a blend of Indian and Ceylon teas or a Keemun based blend, this popular morning tea is full-bodied, strong, and aromatic. Its rich flavor is enhanced with milk.

Keemun - a fine quality Chinese tea originating in the Anhui Province of southern China, this is a full-bodied tea with a haunting nut-like quality to its taste. Serve with milk for maximum enjoyment.

Lapsang Souchong - the leaves are smoked over embers to create this rich exotic tea. Redolent of campfires, its distinctive aroma reminds both Ken and me of the smell of Admiral Nelson's ship moored in Portsmouth, England. We don't know why, but we find a tarry, nautical quality to this unusual tea experience.

He loved happiness like I love tea.
Eudora Welty

Oolong Teas

Formosa Oolong - almost all Oolong comes from Taiwan. This tea has a refreshing, fruity aroma and sparkling nature, and has been anointed "the philosopher's drink". Oolongs are created in other countries, but Formosa Oolong has been given the nod by most tea experts as the best.

Green Teas

Gunpowder - when Europeans first arrived in Zhejiang Province of China and were shown the pellets of rolled young or medium-age leaves that constitute this tea, it is said that they named it because of the resemblance to lead ball shot. Low in caffeine, it has a delicate yet penetrating flavor.

Gyokuro - one of Japan's most highly revered green teas made from only the tender top buds. Mild and sweet, as its name "Pearl Dew" would imply, it is one of Japanese teas that have become known collectively as "the white wines of teas."

In the early 1900s, Mr. Thomas Sullivan, a tea merchant in New York City accidentally created the teabag. Attempting to stimulate sales by mailing samples of the tea wrapped in silk cloth to potential customers, many who received it simply poured boiling water over the bag rather than opening it as the vendor had originally intended. Hemp gauze soon replaced the silk to make the teabag cost effective.

Hyson - green tea from China or India; fragrant, light, and mellow.

Mattcha - Japan's ceremonial powdered tea, less than 1% is exported.

Hoochow - the first of the annual crop of green tea from China, a light and sweet tea.

When is tea not tea?

While the question may sound like a riddle emanating from the head of the Mad Hatter's table, it does require some consideration.

It is important to remember that true tea is a beverage created by the infusion of boiling water and the leaves of only one specific plant, the Camellia sinensis. Western cultures, however, have embraced the term 'tea' to encompass healthful herbal, root, fruit, tree bark, and seed brews in rapidly growing varieties and blends. Well-known examples, all of which are caffeine-free, are chamomile, rose hip, burdock, ginseng, cardamom, and a wide array of mints. The French call these refreshing herbal infusions "tisanes" to distinguish them from tea.

Imbued by traditional folklore of all cultures, (and more recently medical research), to possess beneficial properties, the herbal infusions constitute a whole separate world of steeped beverages. The varieties deserve study, respect, appreciation and experimentation. There are many excellent books on the topic.

How to brew a perfect pot of tea

Bring freshly drawn, cold water to a rolling boil in your kettle, allowing about 3/4 cup water per serving. Do not allow the water to boil too long as this tends to diminish the end flavor through insufficient aeration. Never reheat water. By the way, if you do not like the taste of your tap water for drinking, you will not like it any better in tea. In that case, use commercially bottled waters.

Use a spotless ceramic or glass teapot that has been warmed by filling with hot tap water for a few minutes. Drain that water completely out of the teapot.

Into the warmed teapot place one rounded teaspoon of a good quality loose tea per six-ounce cup that you are making.

Pour the boiling water over the tea in the teapot, stir, and allow to brew for five full minutes. Time the brew. The single most common cause for poor tea is not following this step and erroneously attempting to judge the brew by its coloration. Use this time to get your cups, milk, sugar, and/or lemon slices ready.

Separate the spent leaves from the brew. This is especially easy if your teapot has a removable leaf basket, use a strainer, or decant into a warmed serving pot. Stir the brew to even it out.

Serve it fresh. If you like your tea less strong, add hot water after the tea has brewed. Brewing another pot, if everyone wants more, is the tastiest idea.

The custom of pouring the milk into the cup before the hot tea dates back to seventeenth century England. Until then, the British had only known pewter and earthenware mugs for drinking ale, and were afraid that hot tea poured into newly introduced fine porcelain cups would crack them. The custom continues to this day as a matter of personal choice. Queen Elizabeth adds milk after the tea is poured.

"Sun Tea" advice

Maybe it's because the Northwest doesn't see as much sun as other parts of the country that we're immediately charmed by a beverage made with solar power. Maybe it's the memories for many of us of our first sip of the brew in the 1960s with gentle folk music playing in the background. Whatever the reason, "sun tea" followers attach the same seasonal significance to placing the jar on

Iced tea was invented at the St. Louis World's Fair by an enterprising British tea vendor on a hot day when he became tired of watching customers pass his booth to get free samples of ice-cold soft drinks and lemonade.

Make special ice cubes for your iced tea by freezing a raspberry, blackberry or mint leaf in each cube.

the windowsill that many bird lovers attach to the return of the swallows. Summer just can't be far behind.

Health care professionals recently have raised several unsettling questions regarding the possibility of bacteria forming during the regular "sun tea" brewing conditions. Tea authorities recently have pointed out that the flavor of the tea will never be at its height since the water never really gets hot enough for maximum flavor. As charming a ritual as a jar of water and teabags on a sunny windowsill may seem, all signs seem to indicate that there is now a better way.

Harney & Sons Fine Teas recommends the following: for 1 quart of tea, place 7 tea bags or 3 T. loose tea in a heatproof 1 quart container. Bring 1 cup of cold water to a rolling boil and pour over the tea. Stir, cover, and let stand for 15 minutes. Add 3 cups of cold water and stir. Remove the tea bags or strain the loose tea and serve over ice. Adding a cinnamon stick, lime or orange slices, or a split vanilla bean while the tea steeps lends a light natural flavor.

So give the sunny windowsill back to your cat so she can watch the return of the swallows to your yard, and raise a healthy glass to summer.

Chai

The word cha is the original word for tea in China. In India, where milk and spices were added, the word became chai (rhymes with high). Now at least four Northwest companies are creating Chai. Three Oregon companies: Oregon Chai and Xanadu Teas in Portland, and Sattwa Chai in Newberg are succeeding in introducing the spicy tea drink to the North American taste buds, as is The Chai Guy (a.k.a. Jan Drabeck) in Seattle, Washington.

As Chaimeister Jan Drabek asserts, "Chai is like chocolate chip cookies or lemonade, everyone has their own way of doing it." Usually Chai is created from varying combinations of the following: black tea, hot milk, vanilla, honey, ginger, cinnamon, clove, nutmeg, cardamom, sometimes crushed almonds and even pepper (yes, pepper). A highly individual drink, it varies from household to household in India. Invigorating, refreshing and rich, many predict that Chai will gain converts from the latte crowd in rapidly growing numbers.

Here is just one version of Chai. Experiment with your own:

1	quart milk
1	tsp. cinnamon
1/2	tsp. cardamom
1/2	tsp. fresh ginger, peeled and minced
1/2	tsp. cloves
10	tsp. honey
8	tsp. black tea
2	tsp. vanilla

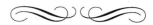

Love and scandal are the best sweeteners of tea.
Henry Fielding

Add cinnamon, cardamom, ginger, cloves to milk in saucepan. Simmer for 45 minutes, stirring occasionally. Remove from heat and add honey and vanilla. Boil 1 quart of water, pour into teapot in which you have already placed 8 tsp. of a good quality black tea. Allow to steep for 5 minutes. Blend the prepared tea with the hot spiced milk mixture and aerate by pouring between two containers. Strain and serve. Store in your refrigerator and reheat or serve chilled. (Try serving this chilled instead of an after dinner liqueur for a real eye-opener.)

A Home Tea-Tasting

My friend Valerie had what seemed to me to be a 'dream job' during summer break in high school. She was a Cookie Dipper, the person responsible for the cream filling in the sandwich cookies. Not only did she look perky in her little white cotton Cookie Dipper hat, but she could actually nibble on her work all day. She was prepared for my envy. I cleaned shrimp on a dock and wore a hairnet and big black rubber boots. Very few people envied that. With a sigh she would give me the litany of drawbacks of her job, although in retrospect I think Valerie was just being kind because I smelled like fish. "First, of course, you could never quite look at

. . . it took her a long time to prepare her tea; but when ready it was set forth with as much grace as if she had been a veritable guest to her own self.
A New England
Nun (1881)

a sandwich cookie the same way again, having known them so intimately," she'd sigh dramatically. Then there was the little matter of the ten pounds she always had to rush to lose so she could zip her cheerleader outfit in September. Valerie proved to me that often 'dream jobs' do not hold up well under close scrutiny.

Most of us lack the educated palate that would allow us to be a professional tea-taster. On closer inspection, the job would seem to have considerable drawbacks anyway. For instance, the tea is sprayed unceremoniously onto the back of the mouth with an atomizer, rather than sipped from delicate china cups and lingered over thoughtfully. Then there's the matter of the required 15 minute breaks twice a day. Exactly what would you do while everyone else had a coffee break?

Having, therefore, eliminated it as a career choice, it would seem that the best way to participate in a tea-tasting is simply for the sheer fun of it. A weekend brunch is the perfect chance to gather some friends, and educate yourselves about the subtle differences in the character of various teas. Here are a few suggestions:

Get comfortable ahead of the tasting with a few of the terms used by tea professionals. (Those of you who are wine lovers will recognize some terms common to the understanding and appreciation of both beverages.) Check the glossary in the back of this book for the most often used descriptive terms.

Select 4-6 teas of distinctly different character. Some recommendations might be: Black Tea: English Breakfast or Irish Breakfast, Lapsang Souchong, Darjeeling, Oolong, Formosa Oolong; Green Tea: Gyokuro or Gunpowder. Serve each tea from a different teapot.

Learn something beforehand about the teas you will serve. Frequently the makers of the tea will have some promotional material on the various teas. Begin by pouring one flavor for all to taste. Lead your guests in a discussion of the varying properties of the tea.

Offer lemon, sugar, and milk; but ask them please to taste the tea first to get the real tea properties before adding anything.

Use demitasse cups, or fill the cups only partially. Place a large, attractive bowl in the center of the table so that each guest can discard the tea after tasting. Empty the bowl frequently - it's not pretty when full.

Rinse the cups between tastings or supply new cups for each brew. Unlike a wine-tasting, tea's flavor is often enhanced by some snacks and sweets that you can offer between tastings.

Variations as your tastings become more advanced would be 'blind' tasting where your guests would make educated guesses as to the type of tea and even country of origin. Another idea would be to purchase the same tea, i.e. English Breakfast from a variety of suppliers and evaluate the blends.

One pound of tea
makes over 200 cups.

Peering through the leaves into the future

Old West outlaw and gunslinger Jesse James was married to a tea leaf reader. History does not chronicle if Mrs. James saw bad omens in her teacup the morning that her husband was ambushed, or whether Mr. James, in a hurry to go out and rob some more banks simply dismissed her dire predictions. He was, after all, a coffee drinker. This simply proves that history, like tea leaf reading, is more of an art than a science.

It is widely suspected that fortune telling from tea leaves began with the Chinese, and like the beverage itself, spread from China throughout civilization. Cultural variations developed, with Scottish ladies adding much to the lore. In the highland of Scotland, the tea leaf reader was called the "spae-wife" (or "spy-wife") because every morning she could spy into the day's events.

Matrons, who toss
the cup, and see
The grounds of fate in
grounds of tea.
Alexander Pope

To read tea leaves, make the tea in a pot that has no strainer. Pour the brewed tea into a cup, preferably one with a plain white interior. The person with the question drinks the tea, holding in mind a question or a wish, until only a teaspoonful of tea remains. The person with the question then takes the cup by the handle in his or her left hand and swirls the remaining liquid and leaves three times to the left (counterclockwise). Gently, holding

Tea will always be the favored beverage of the intellectual.
Thomas
DeQuincey

the questions or wish in mind, he or she then turns the cup upside down in the saucer. The tea and many of the leaves will fall out. Wait a moment for the cup to drain.

The reader then picks the cup up and turns it right side up. The first pattern or impression the reader receives on turning the cup over and looking at the leaves remaining is the response to the questioner's query or wish. Sometimes combinations of images and symbols will have formed, and the skillful reader will be able to discern the meaning.

The handle of the cup represents the questioner. Like a written page, the reading begins at the left of the handle and proceeds around the entire cup. Patterns farthest from the handle are events at a physical distance from the questioner. Patterns close to the rim represent the here and now, and the bottom of the cup is the future. If the questioner is in a confused state of mind, or generally a muddled thinker, then the patterns will be difficult to discern.

The following pictures are linked through folklore to specific meanings:

Bird	-	good luck
Cat	-	treachery
Cow	-	prosperity
Dog	-	a close friend
Ring	-	marriage
Anchor	-	success or voyage
Cross	-	trouble and suffering
Letters	-	initials of significant people
Star	-	good luck
Triangle	-	inheritance
Flower	-	love and honor
Clover	-	good luck
Tree	-	success, happiness
Ladder	-	gradual rise, advancement
Clouds	-	doubts
Crown	-	good luck
Windmill	-	hard work pays off
Wings	-	an important message is coming

I would like to propose a toast. May your cup always hold cows in crowns and birds in trees and may your windmill always blow away your clouds. Cheers!

TEA ROOMS
OF OREGON

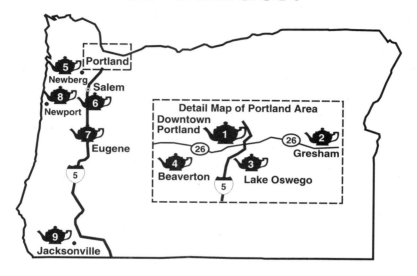

1. Downtown Portland

There are no on-site tea rooms at these locations, rather these are caterers who will bring a tea party to your home or other location.

Annie Fenwick's Bakery & Tea Room

336 North Main Street
Gresham, OR 97030
Phone (503) 667-3768

Annie Fenwick's

Jan Heedum smiles when you call her "a Renaissance woman." She has, after all, heard it before. An accomplished water color artist, wood carver, gardener, writer, wedding planner, cook and business woman; Jan even found the time to home-school four daughters. Even with all that, Jan still humbly describes her life before opening Annie Fenwick's as "just a Mommy." It's exactly that synergy of exuberant energy, style and humility that defines Annie Fenwick's. Unpretentious and comfortable, like Jan herself, this bakery/tea room combination has graced the unexpectedly quaint Main Street of Gresham since 1993.

The scones, from a secret recipe, are legendary in their variety . . . Apple Cream, White Chocolate, Brandied Orange Currant among them. Legendary too, are the special tea events each year that can include a six-foot leprechaun serving an Irish tea on Saint Patrick's Day to the strolling Victorian carolers heralding Jan's arrival in the tea room with her annual flaming Plum Puddings at Christmas. (Be sure to ask her to share some of her Plum Pudding fire stories with you.) Father Christmas, resplendent in a flowing white beard and Victorian gold tunic may even visit your table. Once a year in summer Annie Fenwick's hosts a White Tea that is served to overflow crowds, many in white gloves and flowered hats. It's no surprise that Jan's goal is to be discovered by "Victoria" magazine for a feature article, and it must be just a matter of time so authentically does she capture that era. Since Annie Fenwick's does no advertising, it's good to call ahead for each year's schedule of special teas.

The high-ceilinged storefront operation is divided into two distinctly different areas. In the casual bakery area you can sit at bistro tables beneath the gentle breeze of a paddled ceiling fan to enjoy a hearty lunch or bakery snack with your tea. The menu is varied, from the hearty English sausage "bangers" or Cornish pasty in combination with various side dishes, to an elegant luncheon salad or Cream Tea. A child's menu is also offered.

In the grander tea room, set apart from the bakery by a wooden screen festooned with grape vines and Boston ferns, Jan's daughter deftly serves alternating trays of savory and sweet finger foods. All the serving trays are artfully adorned with nasturtiums from Jan's own gardens. Set amid the Regency period English antiques, the full-skirted round tables are as festively elegant as girls in party dresses. The atmosphere beckons you to linger over a pot of delicious tea as long as you like. Jan recommends an hour or two to really savor the attention you will receive here. You'll feel pampered for the rest of the day. Reservations are recommended, and visit a cash machine first, since Annie Fenwick's does not accept charge cards.

Surprisingly, Jan has never desired to travel abroad. When asked how she could so faithfully recreate the very essence of an English tea room without having visited one, Jan's eyes crinkle into a delicious smile as she answers, "I have a very rich imagination." So who is the namesake Annie Fenwick? Like the unforgettable scones, she too is Jan's creation, "I just liked the name," she laughs.

Annie Fenwick's is open Tuesday through Saturday, 11:00 a.m. to 5:00 p.m.

Black tea accounts for 90% of all tea consumed in North America.

A cup of coffee has 50% more caffeine than a cup of brewed tea.

BRITISH TEA GARDEN

725 S.W. Tenth Avenue
Portland, OR 97205
Phone (503) 221-7817

The twelve-foot long banner high on the whitewashed wall of the British Tea Garden proclaims "There will always be an England." Standing at the entry, letting your eyes adjust, it may be hard to convince your senses that you have not just walked right into the heart of it.

First there is the sound of lyrical Welsh and Liverpool voices as the owners Carmel Ross, and mother and daughter team Judith and Sarah Bennett banter gaily with the customers, "Cuppa tea, luv?" Your nose will be delighted to detect authentic British fare; "bangers and mash," flaky warm pastries, simmering vegetable soup, Shepherd's Pie and bubbling Welsh Rarebit all blending with any number of freshly brewed teas. As you survey the long, narrow, high-ceilinged room your eyes will spy a myriad of familiar yet hard to find British grocery items such as Branston Pickle, Cadbury's wonderful chocolate bars, jams and marmalades, sauces and mixes and teas in delicious variety. Teapots, functional and decorative, porcelain teacups, tea books, tea cozies, and other gift items lead your eyes to the massive wood mantle over the large, non-functioning but dramatic focal point fireplace. A photograph of a middle-aged Queen Elizabeth looks down on you. And what about the sense of taste? You will fool your taste buds too. They will be convinced that your brain forgot to mention you were taking a trip to England. It's all here near the main library in downtown Portland.

Started in December 1992 as a gift shop, the tea room evolved from customer requests for a pot of tea. It has now expanded to include a pleasant outdoor courtyard and 15 inside tables all dressed in their best floral chintz with toppers of pink and midnight blue. It has become so popular with locals that they now offer a takeout menu and a mail-order catalog with more than 300 types of teas from around the world. Special event teas are planned throughout the year which in the past have included Sherlock Holmes' Tea, Tea Leaf Readings, and a popular Celtic Harpist. It's best to call to see what special events are planned, because much is conveyed word of mouth.

Just like the parts of Great Britain from which these ladies hail, there is not a trace of pretense here. The atmosphere is comfortable and relaxing, the service personal and friendly, the food is excellent and attention is paid to the nice details of presentation. Among the house specialities, a cognac-laced pate of chicken and pork; Steak or Chicken and Mushroom Pie; and nine or ten different British desserts. The "Garden Set Tea" is an excellent value complete with your choice of one of seven different types of finger sandwich, a scone with Devonshire clotted cream and jam, a freshly baked tart, and a pot of tea. The homemade Soup of the Day is a hearty meal in itself with the house special Cheese Bread accompaniment.

The British Tea Garden is open Monday, 10:00 a.m. to 5:00 p.m., Tuesday through Friday, 10:00 a.m. to 6:00 p.m., Saturday, 10:00 a.m. to 5:00 p.m., and Sunday noon to 4:00 p.m.

BRIT-ISH FARE LTD.

235 E. California Street
Jacksonville, OR 97530
Phone (541) 899-7777

In the mid-1800s the unpleasant howling heard emanating from the old building in historic Jacksonville were the protestations of the patrons of Dr. Will Jackson, the town dentist. Fortunately for us, dentistry has come a long way in the past 100 years since Dr. Jackson retired, and also fortunately for us, the building now houses the Brit-ish Fare Tea Room. Dr. Jackson's proclivity for cavity prevention may have precluded him from admitting enjoyment of the fresh toasted crumpets dripping with Lyle's Golden Syrup, but he certainly would have appreciated the soft, contented sighs of today's relaxed patronage

The tea room is divided and named for the three countries that comprise Great Britain - the Scottish, Welsh and English Tea Rooms featuring a tip of the derby to this heritage with the McIntyre Tea, the Griffith's Tea, and the Squire's Tea respectively. Resplendent with Victorian treasures, the tea room features an upscale gift shop as it may have appeared when Jacksonville was in the flush of gold fever. The building, in fact, was purchased by Dr. Will's wife Hattie for $600 in gold coin.

Jacksonville is an area rich in fascinating history, and in fact Brit-ish Fare's unusual spelling honors area cultural pioneer and composer Peter Brit. History buffs and tea buffs alike will revel in this pleasant visit.

Brit-ish Fare's hours are Tuesday through Saturday, 11:30 a.m. to 2:30 p.m.

THE GATE LODGE RESTAURANT

at the Pittock Mansion
3229 N. W. Pittock Dr.
Portland, OR 97210
Phone (503) 823-3627

The Pittock Mansion in Portland. The Gate Lodge Restaurant is just around the back!

It is impossible to separate the history of the Pittock family from the history of Portland when it was little more than a clearing in the forest.

Henry Lewis Pittock, English-born, embarked on a wagon train cross-country to Oregon in 1853 when he was 17. Eight years later, starting with nothing but a well-developed work ethic, he had taken ownership of the fledgling Oregonian newspaper and the hand and heart of an American bride, bright-eyed and cultured Georgiana Burton. Together they invested in the future of the Northwest with real estate, railroads, pulp and paper mills, sheep ranching, banking and steamboats. They also started a family. Georgiana's own civic vision and kind heart are credited with founding the Ladies Relief Society to assist needy women and children, as well as originating the annual Rose Festival and establishing the Martha Washington Home as a respectable residence for single, working women.

Mr. Pittock was a member of the first party to climb Mount Hood, and he is quoted on one of his expeditions as saying, "The man who sits down never reaches the top." Henry Pittock apparently sat very little, and in 1914, at the age of 79, moved his family into what is now referred to as The Pittock Mansion. Situated on 46 acres with an expansive view 1,000 feet above downtown Portland, the mansion featured such advanced technology as central vacuums and intercoms.

Georgiana preceded her husband in death by one year in 1918, and their children and grandchildren resided there for the next 40 years. When the estate fell into disrepair, exacerbated by the Columbus Day storm of 1962, the City of Portland stepped in. With enthusiastic community support, they purchased the property for $225,000 and set about an extensive 15 month restoration. Viewing the Pittock Mansion is a must, especially during the Christmas holiday season when it is decorated. It is open to the public for a modest fee 7 days a week from noon to 4:00 p.m. It is closed on major holidays, "a few days in late November for holiday decorating", and the first three weeks of January for major maintenance. Mansion tour information can be acquired by calling 503-823-3624.

Tea is served in three rooms of the restored Gate House, vacated by long-time gardener, custodian, and chauffeur James Skene and his family in 1953.

The four story restaurant, located along the winding lane to the mansion, was the result of the Junior League of Portland's inspiration, in cooperation with highly acclaimed Yours Truly Caterers.

Hours are 11:30 - 3 p.m., Monday through Saturday with reservations taken for 11:30 a.m., noon, 1:30 p.m. and 2:00 p.m., January 24 through November 30. The hours are extended during December, when the lavishly decorated restaurant is open daily with seatings at 11:00 a.m., 11:30 a.m., 1 p.m., 1:30 p.m., 3 p.m. and 3:30 p.m. The restaurant is closed January 1 through January 23. Call for details of special events or to arrange a bridal luncheon or baby shower of your own.

THE HEATHMAN HOTEL

1001 S. W. Broadway
Portland, OR 97201
Phone (503) 241-4100

There is a cute little house on the island where we live, and I keep hoping that someone will be out working in the garden when I pass so I can roll down my window and thank them for the beauty of their yard. The truth is, to pass this house I need to drive about five miles out of my way and then turn onto a dead end spur road, but it's worth it for the lift it gives my spirits. What distinguishes this little yard from countless others is that there is always something different going on regardless of the time of year. Season to season a glorious ever-changing montage of foliage and flowers greets passersby. Orchestrated by some unseen garden maestro, the bloom fades on the spring bulbs as the summer flowers burst into extravagant bloom, followed by rich autumn tones and well-planned winter shapes and textures. To assume it's effortless since I never see human life when I pass may not be fair. Perhaps they struggle with weeds and rabbits, short hoses and snacking deer like we do. Maybe someday I'll ring their doorbell and thank them for this celebration of the seasons. Or maybe I will just continue to admire its effortlessness.

The Heathman Hotel in downtown Portland is to Northwest teatime what our island garden maestro is to landscape. There is always something fresh and seasonal happening to teas at the Heathman. The richly appointed Tea Court surroundings bespeak its 1920's vintage heritage. Opulent crystal chandelier overhead and French landscapes gracing the original eucalyptus paneling set the tone for an elegant tea. The servers, effortlessly accomplished in period lace aprons, offer thirteen reserve teas as well as sherry and port to complement an ambitious and elegant seasonal menu. It could include toasted walnut crostini and crumbled bleu cheese with Oregon pear.

Tea is served daily on fine English bone china, guaranteed in the words on the menu to "transport you elegantly to another place in time, and deliver you back refreshed." Good things are definitely worth a little side trip.

Hours for tea at The Heathman are daily, from 2:00 - 4:00 p.m.

Icky's Teahouse

302 Blair Blvd.
Eugene, OR 97402
Phone (541) 345-3019

Grandpa Mosher would be proud. His grandson, "Sunshine," after a spending spree with the first installment of his inheritance, has put away the flashy Harley-Davidson he bought and used the second installment of his legacy to create Icky's Teahouse. Everything about Icky's is tolerant, non-judg-mental, open-minded and uncon-ventional. This not-for-profit collective is staffed completely by an ever-changing cast of interesting counterculture volunteers of all ages who work under a hand-painted "Yell for service" sign.

The front courtyard is replete with free spirited clientele playing conga drums, selling hand-crafted products and tending the little or-ganic vegetable bed. "The regulars" gather together for beverage and a sense of family that swells in num-bers during the summer when school is out.

Icky's is now in its third year of

ICKY'S TEAHOUSE 3rd & Blair EUGENE

Sun-Thu 10am -12am
Fri/Sat. 10am- 2am

at this point Icky's consists of volunteers dedicated to keeping this space open and available for the creative input, output, cynicisms and silly whims of the community a semi-spastic experiment in creating a safe, class-free oasis in an overwhelming sea of isms and schisms.

providing top quality, organically grown teas and strong French-pressed cof-fee to a growing crowd that doesn't march to the beat of a different drummer as much as it joyfully reggaes, slam-dances, and gyrates to it.

Icky's tea maker the day we were there, Jennifer Japhet, labors a moment to create her personal description of the Icky credo, "It's a safe place to ex-press one's natural, artistic talents. It's about kicking back and having a really good cup of organic tea."

The rules of Icky's are simple: no drugs, no alcohol, no weapons, no hassles. This is, after all, a cooperative whose mission statement includes "creating a safe, class-free oasis in an overwhelming sea of isms and schisms."

Icky's Teahouse features 40 varieties of organic herbal infusions and black teas, and offers a plethora of music, poetry, performance art, and open

Internet access. There is a used book corner with a well-used couch that invites lingering. A few baked goods are offered, but everyone wistfully agrees that "ever since Hannah left for Arizona" the baked treats aren't as consistently good or available.

So where do you get a teahouse name like Icky's? A few years ago while Sunshine was on a bus in Chicago traffic, he glanced out the window and saw the name ICKY'S on an awning in front of a business. It appealed to him, and he remembers thinking "Too bad such a good name's taken. It would have made a great name for the teahouse I'd like to have someday."

The light changed, and as the bus rolled on the wind gently unfurled the banner to reveal the letter 'M.' The business was really MICKY'S to Sunshine's delight. And so, several years and 2,000 miles later, Icky's Teahouse was born.

Open everyday 10 a.m. to midnight and until 2 a.m. on Friday and Saturday.

Up above the world you fly, like a teatray in the sky!
Lewis Carroll

Special Teas of the House

Theme teas for your enjoyment!

A VICTORIAN CHRISTMAS TEA

There is something special about your home at Christmas. The crackle of the fire and allure of candles at the end of a short winter's day, the smell of a fresh tree with firelight reflected in the decorations. All this combines to provide the perfect setting for a Victorian Christmas Tea.

It was during the reign of Queen Victoria that the Christmas tree was introduced into Britain, and it has become the focal point for Christmas decorating in the 150 years since Victoria and Albert lit their candles on theirs. So gather your friends and family around your tree, and put another log on the fire. It's time to share "glad tidings of comfort and joy."

Decor

The Victorians reveled in nature. Use green boughs entwined with ribbon, nuts, fruits, pine cones and flowers. With a color palette of deep burgundy and hunter green accented with gold, you will have captured the essence of an era.

Music

Christmas carols and choirs singing other seasonal songs.

Entertainment

Share Christmas poetry or folklore. Read (or act out if you have budding thespians in your group) Clement Moore's classic "A Visit from St. Nicholas." Issue creative music-makers like plastic flutes, slide whistles and pot lids to enliven some old Christmas carols. (For years in our family Christmas was heralded by "Silent Night" played on kazoos, and "We Wish You a Merry Christmas" usually evolved into a march around the house.)

Favors

A Victorian Christmas tree ornament or a handmade candle tied with a ribbon.

LADY DI'S COUNTRY STORE

420 Second Street
Lake Oswego, OR 97034
Phone (503) 635-7298

Once there was a time, not too long ago, when Lake Oswego was a week-end retreat for Portlanders seeking peace and quiet. Cute little shingled cottages hugged the shoreline or peeked out of the peaceful evergreen forest. Residents sipped their iced tea while gazing at the lake from Adirondak chairs and counted their blessings. Today Lake Oswego is a bustling bedroom community for Portland, and the cute little cottages have been enlarged and remodelled to the point that it's now the lake that peeks out at you from between carefully landscaped upscale homes. The list of blessings to be counted has expanded, however, to include Lady Di's Country Store.

Lady Di's began as a retail clothing store for the fine wool knits and tweeds from the owner's native England as well as Scotland and Ireland. British gift items were added and with their acceptance and popularity, British foods and teas soon followed. Delightfully short on prim and properness, the owner gaily banters with a growing roster of regulars. Many of whom are sure to stop by on the days that May, the owner's delightful 89-year-old mother, is holding court in the tearoom. A popular and colorful fixture at Lady Di's, May works the shop three or four days a week, dispensing wisdom and good cheer on a wide variety of subjects.

Pastel cloths and fresh flowers adorn several small tables set aside for lingering with a pot of fresh tea. Crumpets, cream scones, jam tarts, mince pie, fruitcake, and biscuits can be selected from a simple baked goods menu that changes regularly.

For a little taste of England in an equally lush, green setting, a stop for shopping and tea at Lady Di's rewards and cheers the soul.

Lady Di's is open Tuesday through Saturday from 10:00 a.m. to 5:00 p.m.

While there's tea, there's hope.
Sir Arthur Pinero

TEA & TOMES

716 N.W. Beach
Newport, OR 97365
Phone (541) 265-2867

I grew up on the Oregon coast, resigned to the local wisdom that glass fishing floats, which had been a treasure for earlier ardent beachcombers, had all been found. "In the good old days," the old-time locals would muse nostalgically, "you could find two or three a day." Plausible sounding theories abounded as to why they had disappeared: the Japanese fishing fleet had quit making the delicate blue and green glass balls shifting production instead to durable synthetic floats to keep their nets afloat, the currents had changed, the jetstream had shifted, El Nino had arrived, there was a Republican in the White House. In short, it was common knowledge that expecting to find any would be futile.

Years later, when Ken and I moved to the Oregon coast for a winter's rest he casually mentioned his intention to find some of these ethereal glass balls. Instead of heeding the drone of conventional wisdom, (including mine) he began quietly consulting tide tables, maps, and wind patterns. The first day he found two on a busy beach in front of a popular resort. The second day we went together and found four more, lying like the unstrung gems of a necklace on the shoreline. Almost daily, when conditions were right, the ocean would yield up a bit more treasure to us. I learned something very valuable that drizzly winter - what you expect to receive is pretty much what you will get. We prize those glass balls more than any Chihuly original.

Tap dancing vaudevillians once sought fortune on the stage in the old theater in historic Nye Beach. Summer cottages clustered around the popular natatorium, where the vacationers from Portland and the Willamette Valley would "take the waters" and promenade nightly on the plank boardwalks. In the 1970s when these boardwalks were torn up to update the area with concrete sidewalks, local children turned treasure hunters. Literally hundreds of Liberty nickels and silver dollars that had fallen through the planks and lay hidden for nearly a hundred years were exposed, yielding themselves to the youngsters like the ocean offering up glass fishing floats.

Today Nye Beach is a hidden jewel of the Newport area. Popular gift shop Illingworth's is in the neighborhood, as is the Sylvia Beach Hotel. Less travelled than the touristy Yaquina Bay waterfront, the area appealed to Dawn Aldridge and her family. After researching tea and tea shops in England and Scotland for three months, they settled on Newport because the climate reminded them of Britain and "there is never a day when it is too hot to enjoy a cup of tea!"

Opened in the summer of 1996 in the refurbished theater building, Tea & Tomes has been decorated in the finest English tradition. The ornate cast iron

Victorian fireplaces are from the English Lake District. The original wood floors and beaded wainscoting have been lovingly restored and antique English sideboards and cabinets look right at home as display pieces for the gift and gourmet items also offered here. Books and teas abound, a nice combination in all weather.

Scones and freshly baked goods like quiche and pasties are offered with the tea, or a full Afternoon Tea assortment served on artfully adorned multi-tiered trays gives you a sampling of sweet and savory treats. If you expect to find treasure on the Oregon Coast, you will be right, because Tea & Tomes has arrived.

Tea & Tomes is open 10:30 a.m. to 6 p.m. Tuesday through Saturday, and 1 p.m. to 5 p.m. on Sunday. Teas are served from 11 a.m. on with the last serving at 5 p.m. (4 p.m. on Sunday).

Tea is rich in flavonoids, vitamin-like compounds that appear to make platelets prone to clotting according to Dutch researchers. Men who drank more than 4.7 cups of black tea a day reduced their risk of stroke by 69% compared with those who drink less than 2.6 cups per day.

TUDOR ROSE TEAROOM AND GIFT SHOP

480 Liberty St. S.E.
Salem, OR 97301
Phone (503) 588-2345

Salem is a town that respects neatness and order. Its tree-lined streets are home to gray squirrels that are polite enough to let traffic flow, one small paw gathered up by their chests in an inquiring pose, and then scamper across when the light changes. Manicured lawns and artfully arranged flower beds are the norm on Gaiety Hill, a cheerful-sounding historic district of Salem where you will find Tudor Rose Tearoom and Gift Shop.

The Tudor Rose looks like an enlarged version of a collectible cottage you admire in tiny Christmas villages on fireplace mantles festooned with evergreen boughs. It was, in fact, used as the model for one of Ian Fraser's delightful limited edition miniature cottages. Vine covered and charming, the flower beds and boxes are lovingly planted each year by Mrs. Jones, the proprietor, with more than 3,000 multicolored flowering annuals. Blossoming trees shade the parking area in spring and the cheerful sound of Mill Creek rises from behind the Tudor style, roomy 4,000 square foot gift shop/British grocery/tearoom that British Heritage magazine named to the elite "Top 100 Tearooms of the United States and England." Yes, that's right, "and England."

Authentic in every detail, the Tudor Rose has graced Liberty Street on Gaiety Hill since 1984. It was at that time that Mrs. Jones, formerly of Devonshire, and Mr. Jones, retired U.S. military formerly of Texas, conceived the business when the building became available. The best arts of hospitality are melded in this couple. Mrs. Jones radiates the genuinely comfortable, sensible English style; Mr. Jones, the respectful cordiality of the southern gentleman (who shocked both of them when his first words to her 48 years ago were, "I'm going to marry you.")

The grocery and gift section is well stocked with a huge variety of British goods and books all set forth on the shelves in straight-forward, no-nonsense, well-lighted displays that invite exploration. Whatever you are seeking will be easy to find, and it will be Mrs. Jones herself that will take the time to greet you and to answer your questions or offer a personal opinion of a product if you ask. Mrs. Jones obviously enjoys people, and treats every visitor to Tudor Rose with a great deal of polite respect. This attention to courtesy and service is ingrained in her charming employees as well. Your excellent tea will be served by efficient, well-mannered servers attractively attired in spotless starched white aprons. The menu is broad, with many favorite English dishes like Shepherd's Pie, Ploughman's Lunch, Banger in a Bun, as well as soup and sandwich combinations, assorted tea plates, and more than ten desserts. The baker, a lady from Oxford, England, has tremendous talents. Ask to see the photos of a cake she created in the exact likeness of one of the collectible David Tate cottages on display in the gift shop. Mrs. Jones hand-carried the big cake by plane to Indiana as a gift to the artist, a feat that ranks right up there with decorating it. It just goes to prove that nothing is too much trouble for Mrs. Jones. As her guest for tea you will see what we mean.

Update

As we go to press, new owners Bob and Terry Brooks have taken over this operation. With their past experience as owners of a Salem gift shop for 14 years, Bob and Terry intend to maintain the traditions begun by the Jones' and look forward to welcoming you for tea and a browse through the gift section of The Tudor Rose.

Hours Monday through Friday 9:00 a.m. - 5:30 p.m., Saturday noon - 5:00 p.m.

MOVEABLE FEASTS . . .
THE TRAVELLING TEA PARTY

In researching the TeaTime in the Northwest we were pleasantly surprised to unearth a related business trend, which we will call "the travelling tea party." At least two companies have recently formed to accommodate the tea party in places other than a fixed tea room and open a whole range of ideas for your next special event.

TEAS PLEASE!

9810 S.W. Dapplegrey Loop
Beaverton, OR 97008
(503) 524-4756 or (503) 245-7033

Tea caterers Patty Ennis and Annette Suchy understand that behind the philosophy of tea-time is peace and tranquility. They also know that those two elements can be extremely elusive for the host or hostess with so many details of a tea party to consider and coordinate. So what could be nicer than turning the entire event over to professionals?

Annette and Patty bring to the tea table all their attention to the fine details: linens, flowers, antique English bone china, utensils, candles, as well as the labor of menu planning, shopping, food preparation, set up, serving, all the way through cleanup. The tea party will come to your home or office, indoors or outside. This is a flexible arrangement designed to suit your needs.

Several teas that Teas Please! suggest are the Business Tea as an alternative to the usual restaurant lunch to dazzle clients or celebrate a promotion in a relaxed atmosphere that highlights your good taste. Even consider the benefits of the 'Business Tea' once a month in appreciation of your own office or sales staff.

The 'Afternoon Tea' is a lovely way to celebrate a shower, a job promotion, or club meeting and features all the traditional fare created with the professional flair. Their 'Candlelight Tea' is a three course meal that just possibly could replace the cocktail party for the millennium. Brainstorm with these ladies to create the perfect tea party for your group of 8 or more . . . and then relax!

YOUR HOUSE OR MINE

117 S. College
Newberg, OR 97132
Phone (503) 538-7155
or (503) 281-0001

Your House or Mine

What do you get when you take two high energy ladies, an 1896 Queen Anne style house, more than 100 vintage hats, a sense of elegant fun, and good tea? The recipe for the successful tea party business - Your House or Mine!

Cathie Rawlings and Suzanne Gilliam have spent the last five years hosting English tea parties and are known as much for their impeccable style as their delectable tea treats. The tables and menus reflect the season, utilizing a dazzling array of lovely linens, bright flowers, and fine china. You just might find several of your very own treasures woven into the decor scheme of the table if the party is at your house, as these ladies have an appreciative eye for the unusual and a fresh approach to entertaining. The Victorians would have loved it.

The tea party can come to your house or office, or your band of 6 or more will be welcome in either Cathie or Suzanne's lovely homes. More than 100 vintage hats beckon you to discover the perfect 'chapeau' to add spice and drama to the party. (Who could resist playing dress-up just one more time?)

Fresh hot scones made at the party are offered with fresh fruits, a variety of tea sandwiches, vegetables and at least three sweets . . . one of which will always be chocolate. They will work with you to plan just the perfect menu for your tea event, and make it a truly fun, memorable time!

Gift certificates are available.

Special Teas of the House

Theme teas for your enjoyment!

A GARDEN TEA

Every year the hummingbirds return to our hill, and the neighbors all call each other on the phone, "Break out the feeders! the hummers are back! Ross saw them at his house." Sure enough, in the amount of time it takes to sterilize the feeders, mix up the sugary solution we call "zoom juice," and hang them up, as many as twenty hummingbirds alight on our deck railing. The thrill they inspire each year goes beyond our admiration for this most unique of birds.

Hummingbird wings beat 80 times per second, requiring that they eat every ten minutes during the day. They can hover, fly backwards, transit thousands of miles in a migration and live atop 15,000 foot peaks. They live only in the Western Hemisphere and can perform aerial loop-the-loops. That's reason enough for us to throw a Garden Tea in celebration of their return.

Decor

Pull your wicker out onto the lawn and break out the flowery tablecloth. Terra cotta pots and the geraniums you've nurtured on your window ledge all winter look perfect here.

Music

Just the sound of the wind and the birds singing, please.

Games

Croquet, badminton. Position some chairs near the bird bath in conversational groupings for those less athletically inclined. Provide bird identification guides and field glasses.

Favors

A hummingbird ornament or sun catcher and a packet of seeds. Give prizes for the winners of the games, too. A new hummingbird feeder and five pounds of cane sugar should have the hummingbirds doing back flips.

TEAROOMS OF WASHINGTON

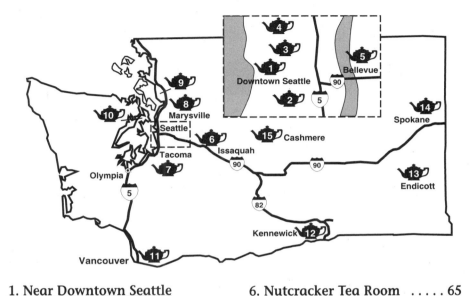

Attic Secrets

4229 - 76th St.
Marysville, WA 98270
Phone (360) 659-7305

If you were pressed to come up with a list of attributes that would be needed to drive a big school bus full of children everyday, surely that list would include patience and a sense of humor. Those are exactly the characteristics that Chris Freeman carries with her to her tearoom everyday. After she has cajoled the last reluctant scholar off the big yellow bus and made sure the Pocahontas lunch box has been reunited with its owner, Chris heads off to join her daughter, Jeni Anderson, where their hearts reside, their tearoom/gift shop Attic Secrets.

Attic Secrets was one of the very first tea rooms in Snohomish County, and this mother-daughter labor of love is still one of the very best. Battenburg lace and floral curtains at the windows, walls lined with old prints and floral-sprigged wallpaper, antiques and Waverly prints, a stop for tea at Attic Secrets is reminiscent of a comfortable visit to a favorite aunt's. This cozy, cheerful, little tea room is part of a gift shop in which you will find one of the most delightful assortments of tea-related and garden gifts, teatime theme jewelry, vintage photo frames, needlepoint pillows, birdhouses, floral stationery and stickers, wreaths, hats, toiletries, books, and teapots all cascading from garden benches and antique display pieces in rich Victorian profusion. The collection has been assembled with thought and tasteful care, (with patience and a sense of humor.)

Attic Secrets is located on a slow-paced, rather bland commercial side-street of Marysville that really doesn't lead anywhere. The tea room might very well have lived up to its name and remained a secret, were it not for having been discovered by a loyal and growing clientele. Word of mouth endorsement of the best kind has fortunately let this secret haven be known. One regular customer, pausing in the entry way before tea with a friend summed it up, "It's like walking through a magic door when we come here. I feel every care and worry just leave me the minute I walk in."

Tea is held in a cheery, intimate sunlit room. The antique oak tables are covered with bright floral prints and lace toppers, and bone china tea strainers grace the tables. Teapots and other tea gift items and lace form attractive still life displays on windowsills and sideboard. Choices for tea refreshments vary with available fresh ingredients, but likely include a homemade soup, sandwiches, and salads (the Chicken Salad is a favorite) as well as the more traditional tea fare in Attic Secrets' Queen's Tea, Victorian Tea, Garden Tea, or Afternoon Tea. All feature combinations of English tea sandwiches, tea breads, specialty dessert, fresh fruits, crumpets, scones and sweets of excellent quality and a large tea selection. The Currant Sour Cream Scones are lightly glazed and crusty on the outside, soft and rich inside, and some business travellers come specifically for them when passing through Marysville. Jeni's service never intrudes on guests' private conversations while still being attentive and efficient.

In the winter of 1996, "the magic door" will open onto an expanded Attic Secrets with the addition of an English garden room setting for tea and gifts. Definitely worth looking for, Attic Secrets is too good to stay a secret for long.

Attic Secrets is open Monday through Friday, 9:30 a.m. to 5:00 p.m. and Saturday, 10:00 a.m. to 5:00 p.m.

Lady Nancy Astor was an American woman, the first woman ever to be elected to the British Parliament. Her countless disputes with Winston Churchill on the floor of the House of Commons culminated in a memorable exchange in which Lady Astor sputtered that if she were his wife she'd poison his tea. Unbowed, Churchill replied, "My dear Nancy, if I were your husband I'd drink it."

The British Pantry

8125 - 161st Ave. N.E.   *1-18-97*
Redmond, WA 98052
(206) 883-7511

I love to prowl foreign grocery stores when I travel. To read labels and speculate on the various uses of mixes and sauces and exotic sounding foodstuffs is one of my vacation joys. On my first trip to England I bought a can of "Mushy Peas" simply because I liked the name. For years that unopened can graced our office bookshelf as an object d'art. While I suspect there may be others like me, you never see "grocery store tours" listed in any travel guidebook. Fortunately, we do not have to travel far to indulge this avocation between vacation trips.

Nestled in a nondescript strip mall on a speed-bump-lined side street of Redmond lies a little bit of England. This unassuming location, heralded from the parking area by Union Jacks, is a favorite of relocated Britons seeking to recapture some of the flavors and aromas of home. Part grocery store, bakery, gift shop, and tea room, the British Pantry is much more than the sum of its parts.

The cozy tea room, which is always bustling, is entered through the well-stocked grocery and gift area. The on-site bakery produces a wonderful array of baked goods, from meat pies to fruit tarts and yeast breads. Ease your nostalgia with a vast array of English cheeses and beers, kippers, teas, biscuits, preserves, and authentically seasoned sausage and lean bacon. The gift area has a well sourced collection of teapots, tea cozies, books, David Tate miniature cottages, Christmas crackers, toys, English greeting cards and stationery. It's a delightful spot to explore before taking tea in the adjoining rooms. A comfortable lack of pretense is the hallmark of this tea room and the service is with warmth and good cheer. The food is fresh, authentic, and delicious. The decor with ladder-back chairs, fresh flowers, and floral curtains is homey and relaxed. The walls are home to a chronicle of British life in traditional framed prints - castles and thatched cottages, Queens and horses, Stonehenge and cathedrals, all blending with copper accent pieces to make a hospitable and jolly setting.

Excellent food in a comfortable, unassuming setting have made the British Pantry a popular spot for tea and browsing for the past 18 years, and will be well worth your effort to locate, as you will certainly want to go again and share your find with friends regularly.

The British Pantry is open everyday. Sunday through Tuesday from 10 a.m. to 5 p.m. and Wednesday through Saturday 10 a.m. to 9 p.m.

Use the phrase "As American as apple pie," around a Briton, and the less restrained ones (like Ken) are likely to sputter "What?! You think Americans invented apple pie?!" (Those with more highly evolved social graces will simply think it.)   In deference to this dispute I suggest we change the term forever to "As American as a tea bag."

Last stop of 5 today. Typical British shop – not much on ambiance but great stuff "to go." Bought sausage rolls, pasty, ginger shortbread, all good. Cafe menu prices high but cute atmosphere (pub).

The Country Register Tea Room

8310 Gage Blvd.
Kennewick, WA 99336
Phone (509) 783-7553

The Country Register
Cafe & Tea Room

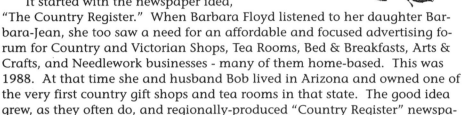

Nobody in the Floyd Family has never heard of an eight-hour work day.

It started with the newspaper idea, "The Country Register." When Barbara Floyd listened to her daughter Barbara-Jean, she too saw a need for an affordable and focused advertising forum for Country and Victorian Shops, Tea Rooms, Bed & Breakfasts, Arts & Crafts, and Needlework businesses - many of them home-based. This was 1988. At that time she and husband Bob lived in Arizona and owned one of the very first country gift shops and tea rooms in that state. The good idea grew, as they often do, and regionally-produced "Country Register" newspapers soon dotted the country from Hawaii to upstate New York. Daughter Barbara-Jean carried the idea to Atlanta and edits the Georgia edition.

Visits from the Arizona desert to the Tri-Cities area of Washington became frequent with other daughters Brenda and Bobbi Jo, and son Brook and his fiancee Beth all living in the region. So the Arizona gift shop and tea room was sold, and the Floyds all ended up living happily along the Columbia River together. The first Southern Washington edition of the paper came out shortly thereafter in 1993 and has now grown from the first 8 page black and white issue to a full color 20-page magazine. But wait, that's not the end of this success story.

Never ones to rest on their laurels, husband Bob had a brainstorm and encouraged Barbara, Bobbi Jo, Brook and Beth to fill the need in the Tri-Cities area for a good quality tea room. (Brook by now had married Beth.) So in 1994, when the big building on Gage Boulevard became available, the Floyds all opened "The Country Register Cafe & Tea Room".

Today teas are served by reservation Monday through Saturday in the country-style setting. The Cream Tea includes scones with lemon curd and various preserves with Devonshire Cream with your tea at a truly reasonable price, and their High Tea includes cucumber tea sandwiches and Brenda's famous lemon bars in addition. The roomy facility houses the Ivy Wedding Chapel where some truly unique weddings have been conducted, a banquet room, and a gift shop, and features a full service restaurant for lunches Monday through Saturday, and gourmet dinners Monday through Friday. The menu by-line sums up the family philosophy "With freshness and flavor as our motivation, let the food be our message."

For information on "The Country Register" newspaper subscriptions or advertising call (509) 783-1620. For tea reservations, call (509) 783-7553.

The Country Register Tea Room is open by reservation Monday through Saturday from 2 to 4 p.m.

THE CRUMPET SHOP

1503 First Avenue
Seattle, WA 98101
Phone (206) 682-1598

In 1907 two brothers awash in riches from the Alaska gold fields improved upon a little farmer's market operating unofficially at the foot of Pike Street in Seattle. Building shops and laying out stall space in an organized manner, the Goodwin brothers created what is today the oldest continuously operating farmer's market in the United States, the Pike Place Market. The market provides a forum where farmers and craftspeople can sell their goods directly to the public. The food is always the freshest, and the presentation often artistic, even theatrical. Today the market is visited by 9 million shoppers a year, many of them tourists.

The market was founded on the belief that fresh is best, and that credo is adhered to with gusto at The Crumpet Shop. Simple fresh crumpets with a light and delicate texture give the shop its moniker, but the colorful wallboards at the order and go counter tell a story of crumpets turned into an artform. You can have your freshly toasted crumpet with Vermont maple butter, or hot pepper jelly and cream cheese, or egg and smoked salmon spread, or simply slathered with butter and your choice of a wide variety of fresh local preserves. Old fashioned "English sandwiches on Scottish groat bread" round out the simple menu, and once again the emphasis is on the freshness of Washington chicken, salmon and veggies. A large colorful cat on the wall proclaims "the tea is out of the bag," and the whole leaf teas are served in a bottomless mug.

Nancy, the owner, takes pride in a counter staff that is helpful and knowledgeable. This little place is always busy, but you are not rushed when ordering. Simple and refreshingly non-prissy, The Crumpet Shop provides a couple of tables street-side and a couple more inside along with a small window bar. Twelve whole leaf teas are on the menu, as well as freshly squeezed lemonade. Local and British preserves, tea pots, and private-label packaged teas are all for sale along a wall opposite the counter.

The Crumpet Shop is open 8:00 a.m. to 5:00 p.m. all week long, but the hours may vary a little in winter so it might be best to call.

THE GARDENS AT LACONNER FLATS

1598 Best Road, P.O. Box 78
LaConner, WA 98257
Phone (360) 466-1325
(800) 767-0637

The unpainted old building with a weathered hand-lettered sign, "The Granary," intrigued us. For a couple of years we would peek in at it through a tall hedge as we drove through the tulip fields that carpet the flats between LaConner and Mount Vernon. The structure's simplicity was punctuated by the riotous rainbow of tulip fields on one side and the large well-tended grounds it shielded from view on the other. Certainly this was a building with an agrarian function and history, but who could have guessed it would become a building with a social function and bright future too.

In the spring of 1996, Terry Van Loon-Craig and her husband Steve opened The Gardens at LaConner Flats in the old granary building. Heralded from Best Road now by a tasteful green and gold, carved-wood sign, the property does not immediately unveil its beauty to you. The well-tended grounds we had glimpsed from the road are actually a beautiful 11-acre private garden. Redwing blackbirds splash in a reflecting pool between two rows of old apple trees which form a promenade to a formal rose garden, herb garden, rhododendron-lined grass walkway and a large pond rimmed with lily pads. Bird feeders suspended from tree limbs beckon a wealth of songbirds, as Rufous Hummingbirds ply their trade in the flower beds. Old poplar trees shield the entire garden from wind. "Welcome to Paradise" - the heading on the map of the garden has accurately read our minds.

The Van Loon-Craig vision for the rebirth of The Granary property includes special event catering. By the third month they had been open they had already booked twelve weddings and receptions for the coming summer.

They are able to accommodate up to 500 people for a full day event like a family reunion, business retreat, or retirement party. An intimate luncheon, bridal or baby shower, or birthday party can easily be handled in The Granary building, which seats up to 75 people.

For the drop-in customer, the menu offers "A Picnic in the Garden" made to your satisfaction from the many sandwich and salad choices they offer. It is packed in a hamper so you can stroll the grounds on a nice day. (Flat shoes are a good idea as the paths are either grass or soft earth.)

The Granary itself is a big, old open building which in its past life was used to store grain for the adjoining farm. Rustic hewn planks line the walls and floor. Herbs and flowers dry from the open rafters, and light filters in from windows that look out onto the gardens. Bright Celtic music softly wafts on the air. An alcove, set aside by a lattice screen from the lunch area, is where Afternoon Tea can be taken with advance reservations. Vintage photographs as well as wedding portraits using the Garden as backdrop adorn the walls. In this area, the tables are covered with sparkling white linens. Antique silver tea services form a counterpoint to dainty flowered porcelain cups and pots on the open plank shelves. An antique steamer trunk holds a photograph album celebrating several weddings that have been conducted in the Gardens.

The first course of Afternoon Tea is a fruit cup, followed by finger sandwiches on a three-tiered stand. These vary from day to day with an emphasis placed on which fresh local produce is available. Ours included mozzarella, with tomato and basil fresh from the herb garden on toast points, delicious round cucumber sandwiches in a delicate mint cream dressing, and a tasty egg salad. All take full advantage of fresh herbs. The scones served next on an antique silver tray are made in LaConner by Georgia Johnson and are offered with Devonshire cream and locally made raspberry jam. The presentation is delightful. Our server Kara was both charming and efficient. Her comfortable blue jeans and easy, cheerful manner signal the easy elegance you will experience here. At the table next to us four girls aged from 10 to 14 shared their baby-sitting experiences over tea with their grandmothers. The Granary has been reborn.

Open 7 days a week March through October from 11:00 a.m. til dusk. Winter hours are 11 a.m. til 4 p.m. Wednesday through Sunday. If you are planning a visit to coincide with Tulip Festival, a call to the Mount Vernon Chamber of Commerce at (360) 428-8547. Reservations for tea are requested.

In 1994, Americans consumed enough brewed tea to fill over 160,000 backyard swimming pools.

THE GARDEN COURT

FOUR SEASONS OLYMPIC HOTEL
411 University St.
Seattle, WA 98101
Phone (206) 621-1700

The Garden Court at the Four Seasons Olympic Hotel

Local historian and journalist Nard Jones described early Seattle as "a sea of mud punctuated by stumpage," and early photographs don't do much to dispute his viewpoint. The Great Fire of 1889 erased, perhaps fortuitously, most early rudimentary attempts to imbue the structures of the city with anything approximating grace and beauty. It wasn't for another 35 years, when Seattleites appropriated $3 million, that this clean palette could be used to create their masterpiece Olympic Hotel, today the Four Seasons Olympic Hotel.

As you would expect, comfort and good taste abound. An enlightened renovation project in the 1980s has heightened the glamour and majesty of the setting, which in turn attracts glamorous and majestic people.

Almost from the beginning the hotel became the epicenter for Seattle tea culture. In the peaceful elegance of the high-ceilinged, naturally-lighted Garden Court, four or five generations have relaxed over afternoon tea. Unobtrusive, yet impeccably attentive service is the standard here. Excellent cream scones, tea sandwiches, petit fours, and tea breads served on fine china fulfill both your hunger pangs and your high expectations.

From Thanksgiving through New Years each year hundreds of teddy bears ring in the holiday season in the Yuletide Teddy Bear Suite open to the public. It's a delightful stop before or after tea.

Seattle has come a long way from "mud and stumpage," and nowhere is that evolution more evident than over a pot of tea in the Garden Court of the Four Seasons Olympic Hotel.

Tea is served in the Garden Court daily from 3:00 p.m. to 5:00 p.m, Sunday 3:30 p.m. to 5:00 p.m. Reservations are appreciated.

HEAVENLY TEA & GIFTS

110 West 13th St.
Vancouver, WA 98660
Phone (360) 693-1417

When Shakespeare mused ".....such heavenly touches ne'er touched earthly faces," he couldn't have possibly known about the exquisite attention to detail that Cathy Loendorf applies to each and every aspect of Afternoon Tea, where heavenly touches abound.

Heavenly Tea & Gifts opened to crowds on Mother's Day of 1995 in a wonderful old three story house built c.1913. Even though the pace has quickened since that day for Cathy and her teenaged daughters, Arianna and Hayley, success has not made them complacent. Constantly testing new recipes and creative decorative touches, you may be tempted to think that Martha Stewart learned all she knows from Cathy Loendorf. The delicate buttermilk scones, presented on paper lace doily on charmingly mis-matched china, are heart shaped. The sugar cubes are decorated with iced flowers, and fresh seasonal flowers decorate table and serving trays.

The Afternoon Tea includes fresh local fruit served in a crystal goblet, delightful finger sandwiches, several sweets, fruit tart and fresh gingersnaps along with the heavenly heart-shaped signature scone.

Tea is served from an angel-shaped pot, and angelic and heart centered gifts abound. The next time you need a little lift for your spirits, remember that Shakespeare also said, "Our remedies oft in ourselves do lie, which we ascribe to heaven." Come and be touched by the hospitality of angels.

Tea is served at noon Tuesday through Saturday, with reservations requested 24 hours in advance. The gift shop is open 10 a.m. to 5 p.m. Tuesday through Friday, and Saturdays 10 a.m. to 4 p.m.

On wings of hospitality, she flew to brew the tea.
Tom Hegg

HIGH TEA

4106 Brooklyn Ave. N.E. - #102B
Seattle, WA 98105
Phone (206) 634-0785

High Tea

Kowloon House

Leo Baquiran has melded his appreciation of fine tea and good food with a commitment to hard work. The result is High Tea, located on a sunny corner of a boxy commercial building in a quiet part of the University District in Seattle. Since August of 1994, Leo has devoted 14 hours a day to his business, a hybrid tea room and Asian cafe, Kowloon House. The cafe dishes up delicious steaming Oriental dishes and either a Light or Heavy High Tea prepared by Leo and served in this simple, tidy, friendly setting.

The Light High Tea includes a pot of tea, a variety of pastries prepared by Leo's friends and relatives in the bakery business, and fresh fruits. The Heavy Tea also includes a half sandwich on a light and tasty wheat bread. Looking for something completely different than your usual tea experience? You're likely to find it here. For instance, try Leo's absolutely delicious Spring rolls and Lumpia with your pot of Assam, or one of his value-priced daily specials. Hand-lettered signs taped to the wall herald tea choices ranging from Green Teas and Oolong to six Black Teas, six flavored Black Teas, and five Herbal infusions including New Zealand Sunny Slope. You can indulge your penchant for variety and true international flavor each time you visit.

Becoming a favorite midday haunt of local neighborhood business people and sleepy-eyed students with textbooks open on the table, Leo greets each customer, many of whom he knows now on a first name basis. There are 11 tables inside and in spring and summer you can choose to sit outside and savor your tea along with the local color from the sidewalk cafe. Intentionally limiting complexities to his cooking and his tea selections, the decor of High Tea is simple, clean and uncomplicated. A potted primrose adorns each scrubbed table, and tea is served from the simplest of pure white ceramic pots.

Leo's only regret is that with the long hours he has worked to make High Tea a success, he simply has not had the time to meet many people or to make many Northwest friends. But as he finishes that sentence two more ladies enter, local office workers and regular customers returning from a European vacation and greet him with a big hug. It would appear that with High Tea Leo has many friends and should be making more soon.

Open Monday through Friday 8 a.m. to 8 p.m. and Saturday 10 a.m. to 7 p.m., closed Sundays.

HIPBERRY

3526 Fremont Place North
Space A
Seattle, WA 98103
Phone (206) 547-7020

As a teenager in the 60's I'm comfortable with funky. Even if I can't define the word, I know it when I see it. That's why I like the Fremont district of Seattle, it too resists definition and doesn't take itself too seriously.

Passing over the Fremont Bridge with the "Welcome to Fremont - Center of the Universe" sign lands you in a four or five block area of creative, unpretentious, and truly eclectic commerce. Coffee shops, ethnic food, hand crafted musical instruments, community activism offices, folk art, rubber stamps, and used records rub shoulders with vintage clothing and lava lamps.

Suitably, the popular community art, Richard Beyer's Waiting for the Interurban, depicts a bus stop frozen in time. Locals for years have felt a compulsion to adorn these concrete commuters in changing ensembles of seasonal wear, party hats, political paraphernalia, and sports team logos. Under a nearby bridge a giant troll sculpture with bulging eyes greedily scoops up an unsuspecting Volkswagen Beetle to snack upon. Nowhere else in Seattle took the demise of the Grateful Dead so hard. That's Fremont in a nutshell.

In 1994 Gregary Reyes, sensing the trend toward good tea, opened Hipberry in Fremont. A wrought-iron gated entry leads to the tiny second story location which is heralded by a suspended teapot when the shop is open. A narrow balcony affords a fresh air seating area above lush greenery.

Two different teas are featured daily, which the shop also sells bulk. A few gift items like locally hand-crafted candles and incense invite exploration. Sweets and crackers are available to accompany your tea.

Open 11-6 on weekends, call to confirm weekdays.

Each cup of tea represents an imaginary voyage.
Catherine Deuzel

JUDITH'S TEA ROOMS

and Rose Cafe
18820 Front St.
Poulsbo, WA 98370
Phone (360) 697-3449

Stress levels seem to run high at espresso stands, and I think it's more than the caffeine content causing that nervous fidgeting in espresso cart lines. I think it's because there is a whole coffee-culture language foreign to most people. Ordering a coffee has become something of an art, "Gimme a skinny double tall, no whip!" they shriek shamelessly over the roar of a passing bus at the corner stand. "I'll have a grande half-half wet cappuccino!" This language separates those in the coffee aficionado loop, so to speak, from those of us who just want a cup of it occasionally. It's a harsh language too. A sign at a coffee cart I stopped at on a business trip in Oregon recently threatened me with "A Slap Alongside the Head" for $2.00, (which to my relief turned out simply to be an extra shot of high-octane espresso in their java drink du jour.) It's certainly no wonder in these fast-paced times that tea is growing in popularity. Tea is simple, it's civilized, it's peaceful, it's romantic, and with any luck at all we will never, ever be subjected to a drive-through tearoom.

Judith Goodrich respects civility and romance. In the introduction to her popular new book, Favorite Recipes from Judith's, she recalls, "As a young girl reading romantic English novels, tearooms and teatimes were always mentioned as part of a very civilized ritual. I dearly love tradition, afternoon teas, fine china, and fresh flowers."

You will find all of those essential teatime elements at Judith's Tearooms and Rose Cafe On Front Street next to the old Olympic Inn in Poulsbo. Consistently honored as one of the Northwest Best Places, Judith's Tearooms evolved from a formal tearoom to a relaxing European style, open air cafe serving lunch and afternoon tea seven days a week.

The only possible stress you could encounter here is in narrowing your selection of totally delicious choices from Judith's extensive menu.

Judith's Tea Rooms is open daily from 11 a.m. to 5 p.m.

Loose tea will keep more than a year in an unopened, airtight container kept out of the direct sun. Teabags last for only about six months.

KADO TEA GARDEN

at the Seattle Asian Art Museum
Volunteer Park
1400 East Prospect
Seattle, WA 98102
Phone (206) 344-5265

There is a timeless Asian proverb, "Teachers open the door, but you must enter by yourself." Flanked as it is by two reclining camel sculptures, the doors of the Seattle Asian Art Musuem and Kado Tea Garden are not only easy to find but provide access to a world of riches in both art and tea.

While admission to the museum is not required for tea here, it certainly would be a shame to miss this Seattle treasure in Capitol Hill's Volunteer Park. In keeping with the city's "First Thursday" tradition of free admission to art galleries on the first Thursday of each month, the Kado Tea Garden has created events to enhance your enjoyment and cultural education. From noon to 8:30 p.m. on the first Thursday you can experience a fascinating range of enlightenment that includes Ikebana Flower Arranging, Tea Making and Tea Tastings. You can experience the exotic nuances of a Bowl of Whisked Green Tea, and linger with the tea you purchase while poetry is read in the evening.

Teas have been selectively blended, many as Kado's original blends, to enhance your cultural discovery. With the avowed philosophy that "The nuances of each country, each culture, are unveiled in a cup of tea," more than 30 teas are available. Black teas here are those from India, Malaysia, China, Sri Lanka, and several English blends. There are four Oolong teas and five green tea varieties offered. The tea menu is rounded out with lively or southing floral and herbal tisanes. Tea service includes your choice of tea "properly brewed in an individual ceramic teapot presented on a tea tray with a tea cozy." Scones, cookies and treats are welcome companions in any culture, and the appropriate teacup for your choice of tea is an especially nice touch.

The setting for tea is serene and uplifting with a bubbling rock fountain and soft Asian music enhancing, never intruding upon, your teatime. In the words of Kado's own welcoming statement, "As your hosts, we are here to provide you a calming, restorative experience; an oasis of reflection and peace. And we are here to encourage and assist your exploration of tea; to answer your questions about tea, and its culture and manufacture around the world. To Peace in Your Cup."

During the summer season, tea is served on the "First Thursday" 10 a.m. to 8:30 p.m., and every Friday and Saturday, 11 a.m. to 4:30 p.m., and every Sunday from noon to 4:30 p.m. Hours and events vary like the seasons, a call is a reasoned prelude to the opening of this door. Your teachers await.

Langley Tea Room

221 - Second Street #15B
Langley, WA 98260
Phone (360) 221-6292

Aunt Marwayne and Ken's mum Emily Lewis at the Langley Tea Room

When Captain Vancouver explored the shoreline of the Pacific Northwest more than 200 years ago, a glimpse of nostalgia accompanies his journal entry. "A picture so pleasing could not fail to call to our remembrance certain delightful and beloved situations in Old England," he rhapsodized. After two years of rugged coastal exploration who can blame the young captain for leaning on the deck rail of the Discovery, gazing wistfully at the view and longing for a good cup of tea?

Today in the charming village of Langley on Whidbey Island, Pat Powell has created a delightful tea room Captain Vancouver (and the more refined of his crew members) would have enjoyed. Decorated in vibrant English country cottage style with floral chintz covered tables and cut-work toppers, books, fine art, murals by her talented artist husband, and abundant fresh flowers, the Langley Tea Room was created to simultaneously soothe and invigorate. Exactly like a good cup of tea. In the outside seating area, the lovely garden courtyard of cobbled brick echoes the relaxing sound of a bubbling fountain.

The menu includes an assortment of fresh and tasty tea sandwiches, salad, and dessert. The preserves are from Whidbey Island's famous fresh loganberries, and the fresh gingerbread is layered with rich whipped cream and jam. Crumpet varieties include egg and chive, veggie patty with lemon mayo and marinated locally grown tomatoes, garden cucumber with herbed cream cheese, or the simplicity of honey butter and marmalade.

Travel to Whidbey is scenic from both directions, either through LaConner to dramatic Deception Pass and down the island, or on board a Washington State ferry from Edmonds. When you find yourself leaning on the deck railing, enjoying Captain Vancouver's view, and wistfully longing for good tea, you now know where to go.

Tea is served 11-5 everyday except Wednesday. It would be wise to confirm this the day you plan to go, since Langley is a flexible environment for creative businesses.

LISA'S TEA TREASURES

10687 N.E. 2nd Street *1/18/97*
Bellevue, WA 98004
Phone (206) 453-4TEA
(453-4832)

During a series of lectures on oil painting in 1836. renowned landscape artist John Constable characterized one particular scene with "all is lovely - all amiable - all is amenity and repose; - the calm sunshine of the heart." Your tea experience at Lisa's Tea Treasures in Bellevue must be something akin to that landscape.

TEA ROOM & GIFT PARLOUR

Since opening in 1995, owner Karen Lund and manager Kemberli Paffendorf have provided a place where people can "slow down, talk quietly, write in their journals, and just contemplate life." Haven't we all dreamed of a little bell in our life with which we could summon courteous and attentive service to our needs? It's on your linen-covered table at Lisa's, right there next to the delicate china, the silver tea strainer, the gourmet foods, and cozy-covered teapot wafting those delicious scents. The era is decidedly Victorian, the mood is elegant and serene.

With nine different Afternoon Tea combinations and nine more lighter teas, the menu at Lisa's is comprehensive, well researched, and presented with grace. An a la carte menu offers even further variety with an international emphasis, including the South Seas, Portugal, Austria, Japan, China, England, France and Morocco for tasty inspiration.

Every available nook and cranny of the five separate and distinct tea rooms of the salon are overflowing with tea-related gifts and books, private label teas, as well as select china and porcelain imported from Germany, Russia, England, Japan and China. A gourmet section tantalizes with preserves and curds, mixes and goodies in attractive packaging.

If it's time for you to recapture the "calm sunshine of the heart," may we sugggest and Afternoon Tea at Lisa's Tea Treasures in Bellevue?

Open daily, Monday and Tuesday, 8:00 a.m. to 6:00 p.m.; Wednesday through Friday, 8:00 a.m. to 9:00 p.m.; Saturday and Sunday, 10:00 a.m. to 9:00 p.m.

(see notes in back) →

Russians drink their tea from glasses with lots of lemon, sugar, or sweet jam stirred in.

The Little Tea Room

105 W. Meeker
Puyallup, WA 98371
Phone (206) 565-4353

In our married life we have owned, or been owned by, two wonderful but completely different Alaskan Malemute dogs. Eric the Terrible was a lofty thinker, gazing into fireplaces and off at distant vistas absorbed in thought. He only had one shortcoming. He hated cats. Perhaps that's what he thought about. We spent the better part of his 8 years keeping cats away from him and vice versa. It was natural then that we would continue dog/cat segregation with our last malemute, Cody Coyotey. As an adult at 140 pounds with paws the size of Marie Callender pie pans, he cut an imposing figure, but he never once had a lofty thought unless it related to sausages. One chilly morning we looked out to greet him and found he was curled up on his bed with a small stray tomcat. Sensing imminent peril we crept out just as they both stirred, yawned, stretched and rubbed up against each other. That was the beginning of his five year friendship with Father MacKenzie the stray tomcat who had adopted him.

Puyallup's liquor store and its Christian Science Reading Room had been strange bedfellows on a block of Meeker Street until The Little Tea Room snuggled into the tiny storefront between them recently. Now tea is served in these cozy surroundings, providing a congenial compromise for the block.

The inspiration for the Little Tea Room was the owners' childhood memories of sweet summer days and stories shared over tea with Grandma in a cozy one bedroom vacation cottage in Deerlodge, Montana. The recipe they shared with us for this book is Grandma and Grandpa's Blueberry Muffins from those carefree days. In opening the tea room it is their fond hope they have provided a spot for customers to enjoy the company of family and friends over a hot pot of tea. Their flyer for the new business states "A cup of tea is like a key that unlocks the past and opens the future." Friendship is like that too.

The Little Tea Room is open Tuesday through Saturday, 10 a.m. to 2 p.m.

Moderation is the very essence of tea. Tea does not
lend itself to extravagance.
Francis Ross Carpenter

NUTCRACKER TEA ROOM

157-1/2 Front Street North
Issaquah, WA 98027
Phone (206) 392-3424

You begin the ascent into the Cascades shortly after the turnoff to Issaquah, and I have long envied its position on the edge of the alpine wilderness. In autumn the foliage takes on remarkable beauty. Forward thinking naturalists in Issaquah mounted a campaign several years ago to keep the water clean in the stream that runs through town and returning salmon have been their reward. An annual Salmon Days festival celebrates their return. With Issaquah's proximity to Seattle, it's not surprising that there are equal measures metropolitan and rural influences active here, and that same blend of influence can be found at the Nutcracker Tea Room, with a good measure of European gentility as well.

In 1986 owner Marga Ilic converted a charming bungalow into a combination tea room and antique shop. Tucked between businesses on Front Street, the approach is by a narrow walkway flanked by Bavarian nutcrackers standing guard under a sign reading "Tea Room and Antique Haus". Cheerful window boxes spilling red geraniums echo the color of the nutcracker's uniform jacket and the candy-cane striped arbor.

With Viennese waltzes softly playing in the background, your tea is presented in one of two cozy rooms attractively decorated with muted peach toned wallpaper and richly framed artwork, much of it for sale. The menu includes soups, salads, quiche, sausage rolls, and pot pies as light lunches and European pastries presented on a tray for your selection are a welcome accompaniment to your pot of tea.

The Nutcracker is open Tuesday through Saturday, 11 a.m. to 3 p.m. blending rural and urban, European and American in the nicest possible way.

Met Marga - lovely German accent - lives upstairs.
Cute outside - not very inside - menu o.k.
limited gifts - new stuff. Limited sweets - fruit tarts, etc.
Would do differently - especially presentation, but
quaint + cozy one man operation. ☺

Theme teas for your enjoyment!

A DRESS-UP TEA PARTY

Little girls and tea parties just go together, and combining that with playing dress-up makes for that much more delight. Comb through local thrift stores for hats, jewelry, scarves, and gloves. Buy yards of feathery boa or fake fur material at the discount fabric store, and silk flower "corsages" and you've got the ingredients for a party they will remember for a long time. Let the girls select their accessories from a toychest or basket, and provide a good sized mirror so they can see themselves.

Decor

Set a low table with a bright floral cloth and make place-cards for each girl. Buy inexspensive marking pens and a paper placemat that you put at each place. Let the girls decorate the placemat with a drawing of themselves as a grownup and let the fun begin. Bright flowers and balloons add a festive touch.

Music

Some excellent children's music is available now, or introduce some bright classical music like Bach for a grown-up feel.

Games

Musical chairs is always a favorite. "Rumor" - divide the party into two equal teams standing in a line. Give the first person in each team a "message," like a proverb or a line from a song. The message is whispered from player to player until the last person says aloud what she thinks she has heard. This is usually quite different than how it starts. "Memory" - give each child a pencil and paper. Assemble some items on a tea tray and walk around the room with for 10 seconds, then leave the room. When you return without the tray, give the party one minute to write down the tray's contents.

Favors

Miniature teacup and saucer. An instant photo of themselves all dressed up.

THE PERENNIAL TEA ROOM

1910 Post Alley
Seattle, WA 98101
Phone (206) 448-4054

Some neighborhoods radiate hospitality better than others.

Where we live, there is a crow that has settled into life here with a broken wing. He is referred to on our Camano Island hill as "The Walking Crow," and has apparently adjusted well to his pedestrian life-style over the past few months. All the neighbors leave goodies for him ranging from stale raisin bread to smoked oysters, and he strolls amiably up and down our hill selecting his favorites from the offerings. In return he has turned our gardens into bug-free zones. Our neighborhood is one big buffet for The Walking Crow. Right before sundown every night he jumps into an overgrown forsythia bush, presumably with a full belly, to dream about whatever crows dream about. With the exception of Eleanor Rigby and Father MacKenzie, our cats, (who ignore him totally in true haughty cat fashion), The Walking Crow is a welcome guest on the hill comfortably partaking of the hospitality we all extend.

The Pike Place Market in Seattle radiates this same kind of hospitality. You can mingle with the crowds in the Market for hours of entertaining sights, tastes, and sounds without spending much money at all. Or, if finding a unique gift is on your agenda, you can do that in real style too. The very best place we have found in our travels to find the perfect gift for a tea lover is located on Post Alley of the Market, at the Perennial Tea Room. In 1990, two social workers, Julee Rosanoff and Sue Zuege, opened their delightful gift shop and tea emporium as a base for their now nationally acclaimed mail order business. Heralded from the narrow Post Alley promenade by the traditional suspended tea kettle marking the entry, the Perennial Tea Room is the perfect place to find an amazing range of tea pots, tea cups, bulk teas, tea cozies, tea towels, tea books, greeting cards, mixes, and tea-theme gifts of every imaginable kind. Running the spectrum from quirky fun to ever so elegant, the Perennial Tea Room has the perfect something for everyone on your list. Two small tables provide a spot for a cup or a pot of one of the 30+ varieties of teas offered as a nice break from shopping. Looking out through lace curtains you can watch the Market crowd strolling Post Alley shops. You will enjoy the hospitality of the Market neighborhood when you visit.

The Perennial Tea Room is open Monday through Saturday, 10:00 a.m. to 5:30 p.m. and Sunday from 11:00 a.m. to 5:00 p.m.

THE PEWTER POT

124-1/2 Cottage Avenue
Cashmere, WA 98815
Phone (509) 782-2036

In 1903 the first wagon load of juicy apples rattled out of Cashmere to eager markets, and passed some equally anticipated cargo arriving in town from the opposite direction. Heralded by an advertisement in the Fruit Valley Journal for Ira Freer's local store, gentility had at last come to Cashmere: "Just arrived from the east...Tea Sets, of latest, up-to-date designs."

Cashmere began as a settlement called Old Mission, in deference to the hand-hewn log mission established in 1863 by Jesuit priests along a small creek near the Wenatchee River. Early chroniclers described the area as dry and barren, but the pioneers who settled here, hardy types like Prussian immigrant Alexander B. Brender, shared a vision of the green and fertile valleys of their homelands. By the 1880s, irrigation systems were in place that had transformed Old Mission into a cool and inviting oasis where fruits, vegetables, and families thrived. A well-travelled circuit court judge, comparing the area's grandeur to the exotic Vale of Kashmir in northwestern India, proposed the new name, which was officially adopted in 1904.

Today Cashmere is home to 2,700 residents, many of them active in the bountiful fruit industry for their livelihood. Liberty Orchards, producers of world famous Aplets & Cotlets since 1918, calls Cashmere home. Founded by Armenian immigrants using an ancient recipe for the fresh fruit and nut confection from their homeland, the internationally known company still welcomes visitors with the enthusiasm of a home town enterprise. Call (509) 782-4088 for tour schedule.

In 1980 Kristi Bjornstad opened the Pewter Pot Restaurant on Cottage Street. Cozy and inviting, the burgundy skirted tables embellished with ecru lace and fresh flowers earned it the distinction, at least with the good-humored men of the town, as being the "sissy restaurant." Kristi's local advertising played on that theme, asking "Are you man enough to eat here?" Many of them are regulars there now.

Special tea theme events abound, including a series of High Teas in March. July spotlights an expert from Totally Teacups at Apple Annie Antique Gallery, also in Cashmere, to speak on antique tea cups; and the local

Episcopal vicar with British roots to discuss the brewing of a proper pot of tea. In May you're invited to share in the celebration of Queen Victoria's Birthday (hat and white gloves encouraged). In August your teddy bear will enjoy a special tea with story time for your children, or the child in you.

It has been 94 years since the first tea sets arrived in Cashmere, rattling in on the back of a wagon, and many of them may even be chipped or broken now; but the civility and elegance that rode in with them is alive and thriving at The Pewter Pot.

An excellent quarterly newsletter of local events, recipes, and remarkable insights is available by adding your name and address to Kristi's mailing list. Drop in for tea, or drop her a note.

Open Tuesday through Saturday, 11 a.m. to 3 p.m. for lunch, tea begins at 2 p.m., dinner at 5 p.m. Hours vary in winter, call in advance.

Yet let's be merry; we'll have tea and toast;
Custards for supper, and an endless host
Of syllabubs and jellies and mince pies,
And other such ladylike luxuries.
Percy Bysshe Shelley

Pleasant Times

P.O. Box 414
501 Third Street
Endicott, WA 00125-0414
Phone: (509) 657-3399

*"The two divinest things this
world has got,
A lovely woman in a
rural spot."*
Leigh Hunt

On a hot August day in
1992, a mother and daughter
saw the realization of a
shared dream. It was the
opening day Victorian Lawn Party announcing to the little rural community
of Endicott (population 350) that Pleasant Times had indeed arrived in
Whitman County.

Endicott is a no-frills farm town 85 miles south of Spokane. Marce
Clements and her mother Jean Cisneros epitomize the hard-working spirit of
the early pioneer farmers who settled in this area near the Palouse River.
Before Jean left for a stay in Germany, she and Marce would seek out
"elegant little places where we could just sit, visit and have a cup of tea in a
cozy atmosphere." During those visits the seed was planted for joint ownership of a tea room of their own one day. A tea room that would be elegant,
yet comfortable; special, yet relaxing. A place where upon leaving from the
tea, patrons would smile and agree that they had indeed shared "a pleasant
time."

Pleasant Times found a perfect home in the charming two-story 1911
house in which it dwells. From the bustling country kitchen to the Victorian
bath, the old house has been completely and lovingly restored with the help
of talented friends. Brilliant red shutters and awnings enliven the snow white
house, and folk art black and white checkerboard painted steps lead you to
the door past profuse red geraniums in summer. An ever-changing montage
of antiques, vintage and new china, European linens, German porcelain dolls
and cuddly teddy bears, colorful handcrafted folk art, tea sets and cups, packaged tea, cards and gift wrap (all for sale) provides the perfect backdrop for
tea. Teas and luncheons are served in four intimate pockets of the house that
seat 30 people. The Main Dining Room, the cozy Blue and White Tea Room,
the comfortable Parlor, and the upstairs Country Room are all cheerfully
decorated in constantly changing seasonal themes.

Reservations are necessary for Marce and Jean's four-course High Tea for eight people with party favors and placecards, but drop-ins are welcomed warmly for a pot of tea and dessert, or a full luncheon from a generous and delicious menu. Usual hours are Tuesday through Saturday, 11 a.m. to 5 p.m., but Marce suggests calling to verify. Occasionally the elaborate seasonal decorating requires some extra make-over time.

The second part of Marce and Jean's shared dream is also about to come true with the scheduled release in mid-1997 of their highly anticipated cookbook.

The next time you are longing for a rural drive, and something a little different for a "Queen for a Day" birthday get-together, a bridal or baby shower, a club meeting, a dress-up party for little girls, think about sharing Pleasant Times in Endicott.

Hours are 11 a.m. to 5 p.m., Tuesday through Saturday, usually. Call ahead to confirm.

Happiness is like time and space;
We make and we measure it ourselves.
George DuMaurier

Pomeroy House – The Carriage House Tea Room

20902 N.E. Lucia Falls Road
Yacolt, WA 98675
Phone (360) 686-3537

The blossoms are bright on the fruit trees of the old orchards we pass on the country road enroute to Pomeroy House. For the last three miles the asphalt road has hugged the bank of the Lewis River cascading through a lush narrow valley, and we are reminded of Wales. With the car window down we eavesdrop on the domestic disputes of nesting robins while carousing crows belt out a song to which only they can appreciate the melody. All the sounds of the countryside of this southwestern Washington valley seem amplified in this bucolic setting. It seems timeless here, probably part of the original appeal it held for Mr. E.C. Pomeroy, the son of English immigrants, when he brought his wife and five children to make the valley their home in 1910.

The Pomeroy House is the oldest house in the Lucia Falls area, crafted into a formidable two story, six bedroom dwelling from logs felled by Mr. Pomeroy and his son Tom right on the property. Still owned by the same family and recognized by the National Register of Historic Places, the estate is now a nonprofit Living History Farm. Included on the grounds are an extensive British theme gift shop and tea room. Lil Freese is the granddaughter of the pioneer Pomeroys. In bringing her personal dedication, gracious hospitality, and sense of order to the daily operation she must indeed personify the strongest traits of that hard-working family.

The Pomeroy Living History Farm is a functioning museum that captures the essence of 1920s Pacific Northwest rural life. Under the guidance of educator Bob Brink, visiting student groups are invited to share in a typical day on the farm. From grinding corn and using a scrub board for laundry, to sawing logs and pressing cider from the orchard, the farm is a learning experience that instills appreciation of all the backbreaking, hand-powered effort that preceded electricity and talking farm animal movies. School groups are invited to make arrangements by calling (360) 686-3537.

The calendar of special events is literally brimming with activities to interest everyone: a huge annual spring Herb Festival and farmer's market; edible cottage garden class; craft workshops that include candle-dipping, spinning, weaving, quilting; an old-fashioned Fourth of July celebration and "baseball game in the back 40"; barn theater puppet shows and dramatic presentations; educational forestry walks; horse logging demonstrations; a functioning blacksmith shop; horse-drawn hayrides; wienie roasts and cider pressing. To get on the mailing list for their "Down on the Farm" quarterly newsletter, drop a request for it in the mail. (As a nonprofit group staffed with many volunteers, a donation would no doubt be appreciated if you are able.)

Meanwhile in the tea room on the second floor of the Carriage House, teas are served to a growing clientele appreciative of all the attention to detail with which Lil and her staff imbue the occasion. The food is excellent and the menu takes full advantage and appreciation of fresh farm-grown produce and herbs. There is an extensive tea list. The Easter and Mother's Day Teas are becoming extremely popular and those should be booked in advance as they are held in the festively decorated old Pomeroy House, where space is more limited than the Carriage House Tea Room. Once a month a special theme tea is presented in the Pomeroy House. Your newsletter will hold the valuable information on these fun events.

The quote under the banner of the quarterly newsletter seems especially appropriate, "When you appreciate and preserve the ordinary as well as the exceptional, you fill in the full spectrum of History." At the Pomeroy House, the ordinary is indeed celebrated in a very special way.

The farm is open to the public the first full weekend of the month, June through October, Saturdays 11 a.m. to 4 p.m. and Sundays 1 p.m. to 4 p.m. You are invited for tea in the Carriage House year-round Wednesday through Saturday 11:30 a.m. to 3 p.m. and the temptations of the family's upscale British gift shop beckon Monday through Saturday, 10 a.m. to 5 p.m., Sunday 1 p.m. to 5 p.m.

Go on loving what is good, simple and ordinary.
R. M. Rilke

Queen Mary

2912 N.E. 55th
Seattle, WA 98105
Phone (206) 527-2770

Mary C. Greengo's eye for detail and penchant for perfection caused one loving, and no doubt envious, friend to roll her eyes and query "Who do you think you are? Queen Mary?!" The moniker was too perfect to pass up, and in 1988, Mary opened her intimate little storefront restaurant under that regal banner.

Situated in a charming single story brick building with climbing ivy and coach lights, the curb appeal of the flower boxes and bright banners have beckoned many a new customer to her door. The attentive service, exceptional presentation, and pleasing quality of the teas have always brought them back. National publicity in glossy lifestyle magazines like Victoria contributed to this urban legend, and the brilliant acquisition of restauranteur Alan Austin-Heatherton as General Manager in 1992 raised the service to new heights. Since opening, Queen Mary has become the acknowledged grande dame of cozy Afternoon Teas in Seattle.

Laura Ashley chintz, English lace, rich wood paneling and comfortable vintage wicker chairs combine to create an ambiance that is romantic and comfortable. Fresh flowers gently perfume the air, and the emphasis on freshness carries through to the produce and preserves. The Formal Afternoon Tea is lavish, beginning with a fresh fruit sorbet. Included on the three-tiered serving tray are finger sandwiches of Chicken-Almond, Cucumber, and Tomato-Basil; an array of freshly baked miniature currant scone, crumpet with fresh whipped butter and preserves, cookies, lemon curd tart (from an old family recipe), assorted fresh fruit and Chocolate-Raspberry Teacake. Choose from 20 varieties of teas. Queen Mary has a small gift and teapot section with elegant offerings as you might expect.

Celebrate attention to detail as an artform. Queen Mary - long may she reign!

Afternoon tea is served 2 - 5 daily, with reservations taken for parties of 6 or more. The restaurant is open Sunday through Wednesday 9 a.m. to 5 p.m., Thursday 9 a.m. to 9 p.m., and Friday and Saturday 9 a.m. to 10 p.m. offering an extensive menu with many family recipes and British flavor.

ROSE & THISTLE TEA ROOM AND ANTIQUES

606 E. Morris
LaConner, WA 98257
Phone (360) 466-3313

John Conner apparently felt the name "Swinomish" inconsistent with the allure of the little trading post he purchased in 1869. Fumbling with the government form that would forever change the post office name, he selected the prettiest inspiration he knew, his wife Louise Anne. Abbreviating to use her initials, the town of LaConner was born.

LaConner perches on the east shore of the Swinomish Slough, a narrow saltwater channel so completely at the mercy of the tides that the flow of water past the Main Street of town reverses direction twice a day. The ebb and flow in the town is not limited to water either. An almost constant flow of tourists visit LaConner during spring and summer, drifting in and out of the lovely little storefronts that line Main Street, eddying in the quaint Victorianism that defines LaConner today.

Typifying the charm of that era is the Rose & Thistle Tea Room and Antiques. Heralding the approach to Main Street, the charming two story house sits back from tree-lined Morris Street, across the street from Bunnies by the Bay. Lovingly tended pots of flowers, a porch swing, and a screen door may touch on your own memories of visits to a favorite Grandma's house, and inside, the tea and goodies reinforce the sense of an agreeable family visit. Decorated with a wide price-range of interesting antiques, botanic prints and vintage clothing, the shelves that rim the tea areas are overflowing with delights. Antique linens and a multitude of new books on topics of tea, birds, and gardens form a lovely and colorful montage.

The tea room is cozy and pleasant with light streaming in through lace curtains onto tables with soft pink cloths, many with hand-crocheted coverlets. Tea is served in antique bone china cups, each with a different floral print. Homemade jam fills the antique glass pots on each table.

Soup, sandwiches, and salads are offered on the menu, but the three tea meals: Schoolhouse Tea, Victorian Tea, and Queen's Tea offer finger sandwiches, scones and sweets in combination with a pot of tea and look hard to resist. The tea list includes smoky Lapsang Souchong, Black Dragon Oolong, and Lady of London among the twenty selections.

Continued next page.

TeaTime in the Northwest

This busy, pleasant tea room is in its third year of operation in LaConner. The owners recreated the successful tea shop of the same name they owned in Claremont, California. The Northwest has proved to be where they want to stay forever, and LaConner is the richer for it.

The Rose & Thistle is open 11 a.m to 5 p.m., seven days a week.

Shelley's Spot of Tea

708 Broadway
Tacoma, WA 98402
Phone (206) 272-7276

When "horse-less carriages" sputtered and wheezed into Tacoma in 1898, many Tacomans looked over the rim of their teacups and pronounced them "a passing fancy." The automobile industry has travelled a fair distance at high speeds in the past 98 years. Many horses retired to green fields gladly in the name of progress, and this interesting area of Tacoma has evolved from Auto Row to Antique Row. People still look over the rims of their teacups, but today they are surrounded by vintage collectibles and antiques.

Located in a four story building that once housed an early automobile dealership, Shelley's Spot of Tea is situated on a raised floor within the antique shop Artistry and Old Lace. Decorated in true Victoriana like a cozy courtyard, many small specialty antique dealers ring the tearoom, nestled behind quaint village storefronts.

Shelley herself was drawn to the world of tea through her affection for antiques when she began attending estate sales eight years ago to stock her fledgling antique shop. Parting with $9.00 for her first china saucer from the prestigious Shelley China Company (partly, she confesses, because she liked the novelty of sharing a name with a fine china), Shelley attended a seminar at the annual Shelley China Club on conducting proper High Teas. Blending the idea of offering tea with her antique business, Shelley's Spot of Tea was born. Every table is set with vintage linens, lace, china and flatware, all of which is for sale, creating an ever-changing tableau for teatime.

Children's tea parties are welcome with groups up to 20, and Shelley's has been hostess to many baby showers, business meetings and anniversaries. Special arrangements can be made for after-hour business meetings.

It would appear that those "passing fancies" teatime and horse-less carriages are both here to stay.

The tea room is open Tuesday through Sunday 10:00 a.m. to 6:00 p.m. featuring four tea assortments including a popular Lowfat Delight Tea.

SHOSEIAN TEAHOUSE

at the Seattle Japanese Garden
1501 Lake Washington Blvd. East

Mailing address:
1910 - 37th Place East
Seattle, WA 98112
Phone (206) 684-4725
(206) 324-1483
(Urasenke Foundation)

In 1959 the people of Tokyo gave Seattle a treasure. A teahouse, exquisitely handcrafted in Japan, was carefully reassembled on a site selected in the Japanese Garden. Later, when our community was devastated by the loss of this haven to a fire in 1973, the Arboretum Foundation, with the assistance and guidance of the Urasenke Foundation of Kyoto, stepped in and built it again.

Chado (the Way of Tea) has been codified and carefully nurtured for 400 years by fifteen generations of descendants of Sen Rikyu, founder of the Urasenke Foundation. The past two generations have lifted the silk veil surrounding this living tradition of the Japanese Tea Ceremony and brought it to benefit the entire world, setting up branch schools in Europe, Australia and North and South America. One part of Chado is known as Chanoyu, literally translated, it simply means "hot water tea." Translated spiritually, it is a ritual of transformation derived from Zen Buddhism and considered by scholars to be "one of the strongest and most pervasive cultural influences of the past five hundred years in Japan," influencing art, social matters, philosophy and hand crafts. Participating in chanoyu requires detaching from all worldly matters and focusing completely on harmony, respect, purity and tranquility in a highly symbolic and ritualized setting.

Suggesting the atmosphere of a secluded mountain retreat, the tranquil teahouse is central to activities and on-going education by the Urasenke group. Membership is $40 for individuals, $60 for families and entitles you to tea gatherings honoring nature such as Moon Viewing and Maple Viewing.

The general public is invited to tea presentations April through October, the third Saturday of each of those months at 1:30 p.m.; free with admission to the Garden. General admission is $2.50 for adults and $1.50 for students and seniors. The Japanese Garden is open every day, March through November, 10 a.m. til dusk.

SORRENTO HOTEL *1-18-97*

The Fireside Room
900 Madison Street
Seattle, WA 98104
Phone (206) 622-6400

Four or five generations ago, cable cars wobbled up steep Madison Street enroute to the forested shoreline of Lake Washington on the far side of First Hill. One of the first stops it creaked to was the Sorrento Hotel. Here elegant ladies in long dresses and gentlemen in hats would disembark and drift through the iron-gated courtyard to spend an afternoon by a cozy fire having leisurely tea with friends. In 1908, when the Sorrento was built, it rapidly became the most prestigious destination for Seattle's lavish events or intimate wedding nights.

The cable cars are gone now, early victims of debatable progress in the transportation system. The stately mansions of the neighborhood, winter residences for many of Seattle's early upper crust and nouveau-riche gold prospectors, have gradually been replaced by a battalion of physicians' offices, clinics, and full care multi-story hospitals, earning the area the medicinal nickname "Pill Hill." But time has been kind to the Sorrento. Inspired by structures of the Italian Renaissance, the warmth and character of this hotel have aged and mellowed like a late-harvest Tuscan wine.

The warmth is not limited to the old world facade. What really sets the Sorrento apart from many other fine Seattle hotels today is the attentive and personal service you receive here. The servers are so genuinely engaging and concerned for your comfort that it's possible to forget that you're not visiting a wealthy friend's private home. Elegant without being ostentatious, the Sorrento achieves that easy balance between relaxing comfort and traditional formality.

Especially nice on a blustery winter day in Seattle, teatime here by the fire will be a pleasant tradition for you to begin, but arriving at the cobbled courtyard by cable car is no longer an option.

Tea is served daily from 3:00 to 5:00 p.m. in the mahogany panelled Fireside Room in the lobby.

(see back)

It is a funny thing about life – if you refuse to accept anything
but the best, very often you get it.
Somerset Maugham

TEA-AN'TIQUES

618 N. Monroe
Spokane, WA 99201
Phone (509) 324-8472

TEA AN' TIQUES

My grandmother Ideala, known to all as "Granny," lived to be 98-years-old, and died this year. She planted a garden and stacked her own firewood every year of her adult life until she turned 90 and simply couldn't do it anymore. I remember the delicious raspberry jam she would make from berry plants she had nurtured, but it wasn't until I became an adult and began tending my own garden that I truly appreciated the effort of love this jam was. Its taste has become sweeter in my memory. Occasionally some well-intentioned but needlessly concerned family member would say to her as she hunkered down to pull a weed, "Why do you go through all this trouble, Granny?" She'd just lean on her hoe and smile a big smile and the answer was always the same, "If I don't do it, who will?!"

That same spirit of joy in hard work is alive and well in Tea An'Tiques in Spokane. Owner Jackie Hayes, who opened the business in 1994, is the reservationist, baker, cook, waitress, dishwasher, cashier and bookkeeper. The job titles just go on and on as does Jackie's enthusiasm for her tea room. By combining her extensive knowledge of antiques with her love of tea parties, she has succeeded in creating the perfect amalgam of setting and style for a delightfully relaxed afternoon tea.

Located in Spokane's earliest commercial district, now experiencing a regentrification as antique row, everything at Tea An'tiques is for sale. If you like the teacup you just sipped from, it can go home with you. Jackie has scoured the gift and antique markets around the country to keep a fresh supply of interesting and fun old treasures flowing through her business.

Tea is served 11:00 a.m. to 4:00 p.m. Tuesday through Saturday. Jackie will be pleased to provide tea for private parties of 8 or more people on Sundays or Mondays as well with advance reservations and deposit. Children's tea parties are invited to play dress-up with gloves and hats for sale in the shop. It's sure to be a party they remember. Jackie offers a variety of options for tea, including a Full Fare Tea with sandwiches, whipped cream scones, and desserts. You can simply have tea with a variety of scones or her delicious tea and banana bread spread with a thick layer of cream cheese, chutney, curry and almonds. The fresh homemade soup of the day, made by Jackie herself of course, can come with a scone too. Somehow I think she must get asked that question my grandmother used to get asked, and I'll bet her answer would be just the same, "If I don't do it, who will?!"

Tea-An'Tiques is open 11:00 a.m. to 4:00 p.m. Tuesday through Saturday.

The Teacup *1-18-97*

2207 Queen Anne Avenue North
Seattle, WA 98109
Phone (206) 283-5931
Fax   (206) 284-6754

Queen Anne Hill holds court 450 feet over Seattle and from Kerry Park you can look the Space Needle straight in the eye. On this lofty perch Seattle's founding fathers built grand homes in the Queen Anne style of architecture for their families in the mid-1800s. While Seattle at that time was boisterous and rough-hewn, Queen Anne City, as it came to be called, was refined and peaceful. And in this rarified air a comfortable community could take tea in their parlors and look down upon Seattle, literally and figuratively.

Today that comfortable sense of community remains and the Queen Anne neighborhood of Seattle is home to many bistros, ethnic restaurants, salons, custom clothing, and gourmet specialty shops compressed into a seven block retail area that invites relaxed exploration. And thanks to Mary Noe's vision you can still take tea on Queen Anne Hill seven days a week at The Teacup, "Seattle's window on the world of tea."

The Teacup is primarily a tea retailer, with over 100 varieties of bulk teas dispensed by a knowledgeable staff in a bright urbane setting. You are invited to have a pot or cup of tea and a scone or sweet baked goodie at a standing bar and two small tables inside, which makes a nice break from neighborhood wandering. The Teacup has one entire wall devoted to every variety of teapot and other tea hardware known to mankind. If you can't find the absolute perfect teapot here for everyone, you're not even trying.

A monthly newsletter called The Teacup Exchange is a wealth of general tea information and history as well as a catalog of the vast array of bulk teas available for sale by mailorder from The Teacup.

The Teacup is open Monday through Saturday 9:00 a.m. to 8:00 p.m., Sunday 11:00 a.m. to 6:00 p.m.

(see back)

*Tea is second only to water as the beverage
most consumed by the world.*

TEAHOUSE KUAN YIN

1911 N. 45th St.
Seattle, WA 98103
Phone (206) 632-2055

Kuan Yin is the Buddhist goddess of mercy. In many classic images she is portrayed lounging on a rock, a look of wisdom and compassion on her face, a lotus blossom extended in her right hand. The lotus blossom, like a good pot of tea, symbolizes solace and comfort. A different Kuan Yin, in 6th century B.C. China, was a disciple of the old tea philosopher Lao Tse. It was this Kuan Yin who instituted the ritual mark of hospitality that survives to this day of offering a bowl of tea to a travel-weary guest. At Teahouse Kuan Yin, the owner Miranda Pirzada dispenses the comfort and the tea in a unique multi-ethnic atmosphere that just may be evidence of her own wisdom and travels.

Rich patterns in Indian and Balinese fabrics and tapestries, Afghan carpets, and Chinese art mingle into a delightful visual blend that serves notice that you are about to enjoy a truly international tea experience here in the eclectic neighborhood of Wallingford. The calming effect of fish lazily exploring the environs of their large aquarium and peace-inducing music further guarantee that you will slow your pace here. Linger and enjoy, because Kuan Yin does not serve tea to go. Indeed, here you are encouraged to embrace the essence of taking tea, which requires that one slow down, reflect, and relax.

Five or six choices of fruit or nut-laden scones are offered as well as Green Tea Ice Cream. Rice paper wrapped spring rolls bulge with a surprising blend of crunchy jicama, scallions, cucumber, lettuce, pineapple and mint served with a spicy Indonesian peanut dipping sauce, and are a rare treat. Choose from almost 40 teas and tisanes from literally every corner of the globe, Kuan Yin's own imports and blends. You can almost hear the bells of the caravan. Teahouse Kuan Yin even offers a Kashmir version of chai, and an authentic whisked Mattcha. Even further evidence of the international bazaar atmosphere is the tea-related gift assortment that includes timeless Yixing clay pots and cups.

Open everyday, long hours to serve travel-weary and others.

Victorian Rose Tea Room

1130 Bethel Avenue
Port Orchard, WA 98366
Phone (360) 876-5695

Somehow my childhood zoomed by before I got around to whining to my parents about wanting a dollhouse. That must have been a relief for them, they never responded very favorably to whining and still don't. As an acknowledged (but unintentional) abuser of toys, I doubt they would have trusted me to handle the upkeep of a residence with frilly curtains for my battered dolls anyway. I can't blame them really, I have never been able to keep lace on anything.

When my favorite vinyl doll with the chewed off fingers, Rusty, met the misfortune of losing his head (I can't remember how, but I think it involved my big brother), my father, who had recently returned from the navy, wired it back on and created a story for me about how Rusty had been working on the railroad and got hit with a pile driver.

While my more nurturing playmate, Suzy Granger, played with very pristine girly dolls in pink flowered dresses with lace that never fell off, and blond ringlets with satin ribbons that matched her own, Rusty's complete day-into- evening ensemble consisted of denim overalls and a plaid shirt. The kerchief I tied around his neck to hide my father's wire neck repair made him look more like a "Bubba," and even now I can vaguely recall he was accessorized with a straw hat and rubber boots that disappeared shortly after he came out of the box.

I choose to think that I owned the forefather of all the "action figures" (boy dolls) that appeared later, GI Joe and even Barbie's preppy pal Ken, but I suspect if I had a dollhouse for Rusty it should have been a mobile home anyway, not even a double-wide. So you see, I simply can't help my adult fascination for pretty dollhouses with lace curtains.

The building that is home to Victorian Rose Tea Room on Bethel Avenue in Port Orchard looks like a great big dollhouse and it comes by it honestly. With charming gables and big round turret in a soft dusty rose color, the building is also home to Springhouse Dolls & Gifts. Tea is served by reservation Wednesday and the 2nd and 4th Saturday of each month at 3:00 p.m. in the turret room. Special theme teas in December sell out early, and the popular Victorian High Tea includes a gift to you of the lovely bone china cup and saucer in which you have been served your tea. Make reservations for your group of 15 or more, and if the weather permits, you can enjoy your afternoon on the patio. Children's birthday teas are made all the more special with tea theme party favors and a menu selected especially for them.

A wide variety of tea blends are offered, with oven hot scones served with flavored butters, fresh preserves made from local berries, rich whipped cream and fresh fruit, a vegetable platter with cheeses and spreads, assorted tea sandwiches and a petite quiche, as well as three desserts, all beautifully garnished with fresh flowers and fruit. Owner Sandy O'Donnel and Tearoom Manager Candace Stephenson take delight in working with you on a special event or meeting menu, so call to get their Special Occasion Planner.

You are invited to stroll through the doll gallery where hundreds of beautiful dolls, many of them collectible, dwell in lace-filled luxury. Rusty would have been happy here, but he probably would have had to be reminded not to put his feet on the table.

When the tea is brought at five o'clock,
And all the neat curtains are drawn with care,
The little black cat with bright green eyes
Is suddenly purring there.
Harold Monro
Milk for the Cat

Village Tea Room & Bistro

17651 First Avenue South
Seattle, WA 98148
Phone (206) 439-8842

There is always a mixture of delight and surprise when a butterfly visits your garden. Delicate, unexpected, and fleeting, it always seems as if the butterfly just dropped by specifically to deliver joy to you personally on its way to somewhere else. In our exploration of tea rooms, several stand out because they were special beyond our expectations and because the serenity of the setting and service were as delightful a reward as a butterfly in your garden.

In the very common environs of Burien, we found one of these uncommon tea rooms, Village Tea Room & Bistro. In an area sprawling with the usual uninspired retail businesses on a well-travelled thoroughfare rest three unique little jewels - the Village Tea Room, Village Manor Gift Shop, and Village Antiques. Emerald green awnings announce these businesses to you from the busy four-lane street that rushes past them.

The tea room is entered through the little gift shop, a delightfully feminine enclave of fragrances, linens, picture frames, accessories, cards, framed prints, soaps and lotions. Through double French doors you enter the softly lit, high-ceilinged tea room. Peaceful and serene, the sage green and blush pink wainscotted walls enclose nine tables for tea. Once comfortably embraced by the softly upholstered armchairs you could easily imagine that you were visiting an old manor house in the timeless Cotswolds of England. The subdued elegance of the decor and interplay of well-coordinated tapestries, accessories, framed art (much of it for sale) and leafy carpet bespeak the taste and care manager Karin Krippaehne puts into all aspects of the afternoon tea. Each table is accessorized with nice touches like a shaded table lamp and fresh flowers, and the richly patterned tablecloths echo the soothing color palette of burgundy, sage, and blush pink. Hanging light fixtures of antique brass, ornate wood sideboard, and antique books on shelves add the old world charm of another era.

Unhurried tea from a pleasing variety of blends is served with pristine white china and silver tea strainers. The three-tiered serving tray delivered to your table by the friendly and helpful staff is festooned with ivy and overflowing with tea sandwiches which may include egg salad, cucumber, and lightly smoked turkey. Cranberry tea bread, fruit tarts, cookies, and chocolate puffs will delightfully assuage your sweet tooth, and the fresh scones with Devonshire cream and preserves are a light and delicious finale.

The presentation is stylish, and yet the surroundings comfortable enough for children. In fact, the menu includes a special Children's Tea with sandwiches and treats made especially for them. Once a year, children aged 7 and older are invited for a special "A Proper Pot of Tea" Party during which they participate in a fun-filled event in which they learn the history, etiquette and customs of serving tea. The "American Girl's Tea Party" features live performances by talented local actresses aged 10-13 that brings to life one of the stories of the popular book series by the same name.

The schedule of special tea events each year is available by calling the tea room and in past years has included such fun as a winter's afternoon of "Poetry Reading and Tea", a "Mad Hatter's Tea Party" to indulge your fancy for playful hats, and a special Christmas holiday event, the extremely popular and quick to sell out "Teddy Bear Tea" and Christmas songfest.

As the Tea Time menu at the Village Tea Room states, "Now, as in Victorian times, afternoon tea is a ritual that allows us to retreat from outside pressures and share in a bit of sublime pleasure." Teatime here truly lives up to that sublime standard, and like the butterfly in your garden, will prove to be an unexpected delight in many ways.

Open for tea Monday through Saturday 2 p.m. to 5 p.m. as well as by special arrangement for wedding and bridal showers and other special events and offering a complete and elegant lunch and dinner menu as well.

When you have flowers, books and tea,
you are never alone.
Alexandra Stoddard

Theme teas for your enjoyment!

BOXING DAY TEA

(Contrary to your possible first impression, this has absolutely nothing to do with inviting Mike Tyson and his pugilistic sparring partners to your home for tea. I suspect that would be hard on your heirloom china anyway.)

In the United Kingdom, the day after Christmas is known as Boxing Day. It started as a day when the aristocracy could award tokens of their appreciation to their servants. Over the past four or five generations, the number of people who can afford servants has dropped, and a burgeoning service economy of delivery people, waiters, hairdressers and the like has been created. The class delineation between aristocracy and servant has been blurred so thoroughly that it has changed the holiday in the process.

We suggest a tea during which you and your friends can unwind after Christmas and express a kindness to those who provide good service to you. Have on hand some small inexpensive baskets and some fruit, nuts, candies, cheeses as well as some brightly colored cellophane, ribbon and gift tags.

Decor
Your Christmas decorations will be in place, no need to fuss.

Music
Bright and lively Celtic melodies.

Activity
Create some little appreciation gifts for those people who have provided service to you all year long. This could be your hair stylist, your UPS driver, the waitress at the tea room you visit, your dog's groomer, or the clerk at your grocery store. Let these helpful people know you appreciate them.

A plain glass Christmas ornament can be inscribed "Thank You!" with a permanent gold marker found in craft stores. Tie it to the package with pretty ribbon to grace their tree in 364 more days. All too often we are quick to react when service has been less than what we anticipated. Boxing Day provides you an opportunity to react with thoughtful appreciation and enjoy a good time with your friends at the same time.

VILLAGE TEA ROOM

7526 Olympic View Drive - Suite A
Edmonds, WA 98026
Phone (206) 778-8872

*...an elegant setting
for a delightful afternoon*

Emerging from the manicured suburbs
north of Edmonds, many drivers are surprised
to discover the pleasing neighborhood shopping area known as Perrinville. Constructed
to resemble a country Victorian retail center,
Perrinville Village has provided a compatible
environment for the unique country craft
and antiques businesses that flourish here.

Nestled in a cozy back room of Village
Crafts and Collectables, Terry and Dave Slater
have created The Village Tea Room. Inspired by
fine turn-of-the-century country hotel dining
rooms, their tea room is enhanced by abundant an-
tiques, lace and linens, flowers and period art. A tall evergreen tree is festooned with colorful antique teacups as ornaments in a delightful year-round
display. Lining a replica wood fireplace mantle, and on every peg of a
clothes tree close by, are some of the dozens and dozens of vintage hats col-
lected for you to wear for own tea party here. A photo album on a table near
the door shows giggling little girls in flowered hats sipping tea. Regal
Edmonds matrons crook their pinkies and look sufficiently prim under various outrageous bonnets. Contemporary gentlemen in battered top hats strike
an elegant posture for the camera, and you are left to wonder, what is it
about hats that turn us into someone else? It's a fun, relaxed , yet elegant,
setting for your tea which includes assorted sandwiches, delicious sweet
cream scones with your choice of topping, Scottish shortbread, assorted tea
breads, muffins, cookies and pastries that vary weekly. And, of course, your
choice of a delicious pot of tea.

*Open for teas and good fun Tuesday through Saturday noon to 4:00 p.m. by
reservations only. It's a great place for parties and for introducing children to the
delights of tea. Be sure to call ahead to book space.*

*Ecstacy is a glass full of tea
and a piece of sugar in the mouth.*
Alexander Pushkin

THE WELLINGTON

4869 Rainier Avenue South
Seattle, WA 98118
Phone (206) 722-8571

The Wellington is located along a maple tree-lined street in a dignified looking brick building that was built in 1910 to house a pharmacy and soda fountain. A neon teapot in the window proclaims the structure's newest incarnation as a tea room and gift shop. The big, old vintage 1920s clock tower on the block reminds us that it's always teatime somewhere.

Gwyn Baker, the owner, has created a comfortable blend of easy southern hospitality and formal Victorian style at the Wellington. French doors lead from the country Victorian gift and antique shop to the tea room, which is decorated with floral wallpaper and deep hunter green. Servers, attired in true Victorian dress, attend at elegant tables each decorated for a different

Tea Time at
The Wellington

theme. Topiary and antiques complete the setting which combined to induce the National Association of Mayors to award Gwyn their Small Business of the Year award.

Afternoon tea is by reservation, and special teas are being poured to ever-expanding crowds, especially the Mother-Daughter Tea and the Victorian Elegant Tea. Weekend breakfast service began recently, and begins serving at 7:00 a.m. It's a good idea to confirm hours and to reserve space for tea.

The Wellington's hours for tea are 3:00 p.m. to 9:00 p.m., Monday through Friday; Saturday 11 a.m. to 5 p.m. and Sunday by reservation only.

Come oh come ye tea-thirsty restless ones . . .
the kettle boils, bubbles and sings musically.
Rabindranath Tagore

WINDSOR GARDEN TEA ROOM

110 Fourth Avenue North
Edmonds, WA 98020
Phone (206) 712-1387

It has long been noted that teatime has a healing aspect to it, so it seemed especially appropriate when the Windsor Garden Tea Room made its home in a charming old doctor's office in Edmonds last year. Heralded by the MD symbol in mosaic on the entryway, there is no mistaking that this was destined to be a house of healing.

Owned and operated by energetic Libby Hustler, the immediate success of the Windsor Garden delighted her but came as no surprise to those who know the energy she invested, (she really lives up to her last name). Welcoming the help of her entire family, Libby decorated the five-room, 1936-vintage brick building in true Victorian style. With wainscoting as a counterpoint to richly patterned pastel rose wallpaper, lace curtains to filter the abundant sunlight, Bach playing softly, and fresh flowers on every table, the essence of a Victorian tea room was captured in Libby's Garden Room completely. English bone china, charmingly mismatched (and many collectible) look right at home on freshly pressed eggshell and mauve linens. A glass door opens onto a well-tended summer garden for outdoor teas. The gift shop features a wide variety of imported and local tea blends as well as books, cards, tea-theme gifts and estate sale antique china.

Special events are held throughout the year, with English Garden Parties in the summer in conjunction with neighboring Little House of Herbs and holiday events, so call for details of how to get on the mailing list to learn of events. Private tea parties for bridal and baby showers as well as children's tea parties are welcome with advance reservations.

Tea is served Monday through Saturday with the selection varying with the very freshest of available ingredients. A Finger Sandwich Sampler platter often includes ham with pineapple cream cheese, a delicious olive spread, fresh vine-ripened tomatoes with pesto cream cheese and fresh herbs, or local salmon with herb cream cheese. House desserts are rich and change daily, and English cream scones are served as well as "American Scones" chock full of healthful fruits, nuts, and whole grains. Like so many of the good doctor's patients over the years, when you walk out of the Windsor Garden Tea Room into the fresh sea breeze blowing up from the Edmonds ferry dock, you might just notice that you feel a whole lot better than when you went in.

Windsor Garden Tea Room is open Monday through Saturday, 10 a.m. to 5 p.m.

The Woodmark Hotel

1200 Carillon Point
Kirkland, WA 98033
Phone (206) 822-3700
        (206) 803-5595

Kirkland's hillside was once clothed by ancient widespread forests. City dwellers from Seattle would make the weekend crossing by steamboat in the early 1900s to the verdant Kirkland shoreline for communion with nature and lake-shore relaxation. Today a fast-paced, four-lane floating bridge unites Kirkland and Seattle blurring the distinction between city and retreat, and yet Kirkland retains the casual appeal of a lake-side village with a lavish dose of urban elegance and worldliness. Nowhere is that combination more evident than at the Woodmark Hotel on Carillon Point.

The Woodmark Hotel holds the distinction of being the only hotel located on the lengthy and convoluted shoreline of metropolitan Lake Washington. Intimate, by hotel standards, with 100 beautifully-appointed guest rooms, it is at the same time imposing due to its location. The four-story Woodmark presides with an air of businesslike authority over the 30-acre lake front that includes marina, pier, gardens, waterfront promenade and salmon stream. Wherever the eye turns it catches the glint of water.

Afternoon Tea is served daily on fine Lenox China in a comfortable, book-lined nook known as The Library Room. As their tea menu indicates, "Afternoon Tea at The Woodmark Hotel offers a continuation of the European custom of taking mid-afternoon respites between rounds of shopping, business appointments or simply to treat yourself to a small whim." The service is impeccable and thoughtful, and the setting is elegant and restful.

In addition to six tea blends and herbal tissanes from local blenders Barnes & Watson Fine Teas to ponder, you can also make your tea a truly festive occasion by adding a glass of sparkling wine, Champagne, or sherry. Three different tea menus are offered, a Full Tea with savories, sweets, and scone; Savories and Tea with a fruit scone without the sweets; and Sweets and Tea which is exactly as rich and yummy as it sounds. For children under the age of 12, a special afternoon tea is prepared that includes childhood favorites P.B. & J. and Egg Salad.

The Woodmark's quiet charm and attention to creature comforts make their teatime a special treat. Once again, as in years past, Kirkland offers a soothing retreat for the jangled sensibilities of urban dwellers.

Tea is served daily between 2:00 and 4:00 p.m., reservations are appreciated.

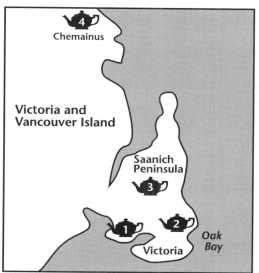

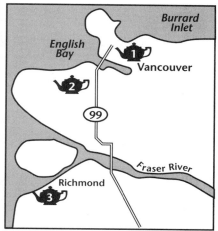

TEAROOMS
OF BRITISH COLUMBIA

Adrienne's Tea Garden

at Mattick's Farm
5325 Cordova Bay Road
Victoria, B.C.
Phone (604)658-1535

Farmer Bill Mattick's portrait in oils hangs in the entry to Mattick's Farm. In it Bill smiles proudly around a slim cigar, glowing with paternal pride at the two enormous cauliflowers he cradles with his one good hand and the hook that replaces the missing one. In his wool buffalo plaid shirt he looks folksy and colorful, probably brimming with advice on fertilizer and good common sense. Obviously he is a man with stories to tell and earthy wisdom to impart.

Today Mattick's Farm is a local landmark on the well-travelled scenic route from the Swartz Bay ferry terminal heading to Victoria. As folksy and colorful as Bill himself, Mattick's Farm houses a garden center and nursery, gift shop, florist, craft store, and Adrienne's Tea Garden. Farmer Bill has been gone for years, but his vision of abundance on this plot of land surpasses cauliflowers, and is his legacy to the merchants thriving here. What could be better on a weekend morning in spring than to stroll a nursery rife with perennials and then revel in the baked goods of a delightful country tea room?

Adrienne's Tea Garden owner Fay Hextall provides a comfortable, uncomplicated setting perfect for relaxing over tea. Here you can choose Fay's "High Tea" of finger sandwiches, assorted dainties, delicious raisin scone with Devonshire cream and homemade preserves, ice cream or fruit cup. If that sounds a little too abundant, you can opt for any of a vast array of fresh baked goods with your tea, such as sticky buns, cheese scones, apple or cherry turnovers, butter tarts, streudel, Nanaimo bars, Eccles cakes, bagels, brownies, apple crisp, apple almond cake spiked with rum and cream or one of seven different varieties of muffins. There are sausages in puff pastry, salmon in puff pastry, and ten different rich dairy fresh ice creams. Did we mention carrot cake and cheesecake? All are created on site with a nod to Farmer Bill's penchant for abundance with the freshest local ingredients.

Since Farmer Bill spent the greater part of his life supplying fresh produce and flowers to Vancouver Islanders, it seems especially appropriate that country crafts, flowers, gifts, and bakers grow on his property today. Open for breakfast, lunch, and Afternoon Tea.

Hours: 9:00 a.m. to 5:00 p.m. with Afternoon Tea available from 11:30 a.m.

THE BLETHERING PLACE

**2250 Oak Bay Avenue
Victoria, B.C.
Phone (604) 598-1413**

To describe The Blethering Place in purely physical terms seems somehow to miss the point We could describe it as enduringly charming, because it certainly is, being the oldest building in Victorian Oak Bay Village. We could tell you about the care and eccentric sense of humor that has gone into the collection of old toys, books and prints that cover the bookshelves and panelled walls of this former grocery and post office building. It all coalesces to create an inviting air of authenticity to the British hospitality here. We could describe the personal, friendly service and relaxed informality that allows hours to slip away uncounted in good company. While all this would be true, it still wouldn't capture the heart and soul of this place, for that lies in the story of owner Ken Agate, and that story is best told by his clientele.

In 1981 Ken Agate arrived in British Columbia from his home in New Zealand and set about creating a comfortable haven for locals. With many of the same Oak Bay Villagers still visiting daily, The Blethering Place is a meeting ground where good company and good tea often brew together. Ken now lives above the shop with a menagerie of collectible teddy bears that perch along the window ledges spying down on the Oak Bay street scene. On the day we visited, we were treated to introductions to many of the teatime regulars, all willing to share a funny or touching story.

At one table were two wonderfully colorful retirees, Freda and Valentine, from the profession of social work. Their vivid purple blouses and flowered hats mirroring the gaiety and enthusiasm with which these two embrace life, and their affection for owner Agate is heartfelt and reciprocal. They are quick to point out that Ken Agate never allows a Christmas Day to pass without offering a dinner with all the trimmings to any and all who come by. On many summer weekend evenings, you learn, the entertainment in the tea house will be a rousing and nostalgic songfest of music from the 40s hammered out on the old upright piano in the corner and an invitation for all to share the microphone with their own personal memories of their youth at the end of World War II.

The enchanting young woman in the broad-brimmed hat with a rose in the hatband sits sipping tea with her long flowing skirt billowing in the breeze of the open door. With a little wave to the other tables in passing she is off again to narrate the next double decker bus tour of the area on the Oak Bay Explorer. Only then do you learn she was at one time in the not so distant past, homeless with no job skills and little hope when hired by the Blethering Place. The work skills she sharpened in this supportive environment enabled her to grow into the wonderful public contact job in which she now thrives.

The Blethering Place offers a complete menu for breakfast, lunch and dinner in addition to Afternoon Tea. Here, as in the decor and service, much emphasis is placed on British foods - Guinness Ale basted chicken, Shepherd's Pie, Fawlty Towers Loin of Pork (with Basil sauce), Yorkshire Pudding - it's a fun eclectic mix as you would expect.

When the original quarters became a bit cramped for all the locals and tourists, Agate organized a work party after the close of business and arming all with sledge hammers, proceeded to enlarge the Blethering Place by knocking through a wall. It seems every table has a story to tell or a memory to share, with the common theme that this is indeed a magical spot.

'Blethering' is Scottish for 'senseless talking', but the pleasant interlude that awaits you here makes a great deal of sense to me.

Hours at Blethering Place for Afternoon Tea are 11 a.m. to 6:30 p.m.

Polly, put the kettle on, we'll all have tea.
Charles Dickens
Barnaby Ridge

BON TON PASTRY & CONFECTIONERY

874 Granville
Vancouver, B.C.
Phone (604) 681-3058

Tradition often improves with age. The Bon Ton is primarily a fine bakery and confectionery in the truest European tradition. About sixty years ago Italian-born Mr. Notte with his French-born bride opened the business, and the spatula has been passed to younger generations of Nottes to continue their standards of excellence. Continue it they have, and the art of baking has scaled new heights under their tutelage.

Entering Bon Ton you are flanked by glass display cases forming a corridor of compelling calories. Rich pastries, layer cakes, Florentines, meringue tarts, eclairs, marzipan, fruit tortes, truffles . . . the menu reads like a litany of guilty pleasures, and what a sinful treat they are. The walls are adorned, not with departed Notte family members, but with framed photos of cakes that have come and gone. Gone but not forgotten, no doubt. The ceilings are high, the decor simple so not to conflict with the elaborate pastries perhaps, and the mood European.

If you came to Bon Ton expecting a wide variety of teas, you would be disappointed. Your disappointment should be short-lived, however, just like your diet, once you perk yourself up with any of the myriad of delectable treats. In an area formed by simple garden lattice walls you will find 18 wrought iron bistro tables in a Mediterranean theme decor. Servers will leave before you a simple glass-domed tray containing at least 12 different creamy treats. How many are left when you are done with your pot of tea may be another issue entirely.

It doesn't take a fortune-teller to let you know you could easily pile on the calories here, but they do have a resident fortune teller (tea leaves or tarot cards) you can engage for a fee.

Bon Ton is open Tuesday through Saturday, 9:30 a.m. to 6:00 p.m. with tea served until 4:30 p.m. each day.

*Canadians drink more than three times as
much tea per person as Americans.*

Theme teas for your enjoyment!

COME AS YOUR FAVORITE ENGLISH PERSON

One of the best tea parties we ever had was one in which the guests were instructed to come dressed as their favorite English person. Margaret Thatcher rubbed shoulders with King Arthur, respendent in bathrobe with sword and crown. Charlie Chaplin held long conversations with Sherlock Holmes, while Fergie and Joan Collins boogied with everyone. King James brought his Bible, reminding all that he was "500 years on the best seller list," and a "Bobby" maintained order while Camilla-Parker Bowles snuggled with Prince Charles. After the party had started, our attention was drawn to the street as 78-year-old Aunt Marwayne arrived. Dressed head to toe in pink chiffon, flowered hat, and pearls, her white-gloved hand waved regally to the crowd as Queen Elizabeth II, fashionably late and escorted by a dapper Prince Phillip. It was silly, easy and fun.

Decor
Small Union Jacks tucked in English ivy topiary with red, white and blue ribbons.

Music
The Beatles, Elton John, Eric Clapton, English choral music, the list is endless.

Games
Croquet on the lawn, Badminton or "Pin the crown on the Monarch."

Favors
Union Jack flags, Cadbury chocolate. Give prizes for the best costumes, too, like a gift certificate to your favorite tea room, a fancy tea tin or a copy of this book!

BRITISH HOME

3986 Moncton at #1 Road
Steveston Village
Richmond, B.C.
Phone (604) 274-2261

On a warm morning in July of 1889, the 200-foot clipper ship, Titania, pushed off from the sleepy fishing village of Steveston under full sail. With a rich history in the tea trade, the vessel was now riding the winds of its rebirth as a freighter for another precious cargo - Fraser River salmon bound for the dinner tables of England.

This aging dowager's cargo was so well received in England that increased demand for salmon resulted in a dozen canneries opening in rapid succession. A "boomtown" atmosphere engulfed this once quiet tip of Lulu Island in southern British Columbia, and weekends would find the village swelling to 10,000 rough and tumble inhabitants. Enterprises that feed on a quick flush of money soon followed; gambling halls, saloons, and houses of ill-repute thrived along these shores of the Fraser River. Every Saturday night the Salvation Army band would parade along Moncton Street, admonishing with a flourish of a tambourine and a spirited bugle that fishermen and cannery workers' souls could be saved if they would just go home for the evening. Whether the advice was heeded is not chronicled.

Today the six-square-block area that constitutes the hub of Historic Steveston Village's commercial district is still bustling as it experiences its own rebirth as a "boomtown" in a new venue. Today's crowds are a better-mannered group presumably, happily partaking in the new enterprises that have cropped up to meet their needs. Gift shops, nautical bookstores, antique stores, seafood vendors, museum, T-shirt kiosks, Canadian crafts, street musicians, and more than three dozen restaurants and sidewalk cafes offer something for everyone by this busy harbor. One of the more unique businesses, delighting local expatriates and tourists alike, is British Home.

British Home authentically replicates every detail of the friendly corner store found all over Britain. Its cheerful proprietors, Mary and Ray Carter, stock a complete array of British groceries and meats, and offer some cooked food from recipes of their homeland in a variety of meat pies, sausage rolls, pasties, haggis, and black pudding that you request at the counter. Four tables by the window, covered in blue smocked gingham with captain's chairs, allow a break for good, strong tea under the regal countenance of framed members of the Royal Family. This engaging couple dispenses tea with affable good humor, and genuine friendliness in a comfortable setting. The bonneted ghosts of Salvation Army paraders must be smiling on this proper British business. Certainly they drank a lot of tea in their day.

British Home is open Tuesday through Saturday, 11:00 a.m. to 6:00 p.m. and Sunday from 1:00 p.m. to 5:00 p.m.

The Butchart Gardens

800 Benvenuto Avenue
Brentwood Bay, B.C.

Tea reservations (604) 652-8222
Garden information (604) 652-4422
Recorded information (604) 652-5256

There is a playful irony in the fact that the Butcharts earned their fortune with a product that is lifeless, gray, flat and boring. Those are certainly not descriptive of any aspect of their life when their cement business was thriving in the early 1900s, nor their masterpiece garden legacy today.

On the 130-acre site of an abandoned quarry on the shores of a picturesque inlet 13 miles north of Victoria on Vancouver Island, the Butcharts built their home, "Benvenuto," the Italian word for "welcome". To grace the naturally verdant setting, Mrs. Butchart ventured to plant her first rose bush and some sweet peas. From this simple act of horticultural, a dormant love of gardening sprouted, and over the next few years of nurturing Mrs. Butchart grew one of the most splendid gardens in North America, a garden masterpiece of world renown.

From the beginning, an almost constant flow of gardening enthusiasts were welcomed to the estate. With gracious hospitality the Butcharts saw to it that tea was always offered. In 1915 alone, it is reported that tea was served to 18,000, and it was not uncommon for strangers strolling the grounds to be invited to the family table for dinner and pleasant conversation.

Today, not only is Jenny Foster Butchart's glorious garden thriving, but that same spirit of gracious hospitality is as well. Afternoon Tea, in the Dining Room is lavish. It begins with fresh fruit cups with citrus yogurt cream, followed by a selection of delicate tea sandwiches that may include watercress and ginger cream cheese, smoked salmon mousse roll, egg salad with fresh spinach, Roma tomato and pesto, and edible flowers with lemon cream cheese. A plate of sweets that may include apple strudel, banana date loaf, chocolate brandy Napoleon slice, and a double chocolate dipped strawberry, as well as their delectably-light, candied ginger scone with whipped vanilla Devon cream. Manager Richard Schmidt sees to it that a large tea selection is offered. The presentation is at once formal and attentive, and the surroundings are impeccable with masses of beautiful fresh flowers gracing the antique-laden room.

Allow plenty of time to explore these glorious gardens. Internationally acclaimed, there is something special and unique about them at every season

The Butchart Residence - Summer.   Courtesy of the Butchart Gardens Ltd.

of the year. During summer evenings, thousands of gently colored lights create a mystical setting for outdoor musical performances and sing-alongs.

Fireworks with musical accompaniment rival the brilliance of the blooms on some summer nights. In winter a special magic prevails with strolling carollers singing traditional tunes on crisp December days. Comfortable benches invite peaceful contemplation of the changing beauty of the gardens at all times of the year.

The estate was aptly named, Benvenuto. As in the days when Jenny Butchart approached guests in her garden to come in for tea, the tea room is offered as a service for today's garden visitors. As such, you will need to pay the reasonable admission price to enter the grounds where the tea room is located. Once there, you will, like countless international visitors for the past 92 years, feel very welcome in this glorious setting, a tribute to all that is good about warm hospitality and superior horticulture.

Tea is served seasonally 1 p.m. to 4 p.m. Please call (604) 652-8222 for reservations. Admission fee for garden is required for access to the tea room.

Like plants, most men have hidden properties
that chance alone reveals.
La Rochefoucauld
Maxims

The Captain's Palace Inn

309 Belleville Street
Victoria, B.C.
Phone (604) 388-9191

William Pendray made a promise to his new bride, Amelia. When they made their fortune, he said, he would build her a home that would rival the "painted ladies," the elaborate Queen Anne style houses she had admired in 1877 on their honeymoon in San Francisco. It took 20 years, but Mr. Pendray was true to his word. Laboring intently at his soap and paint business he was able to afford a grand family home for his love Amelia and their four sons on Belleville Street overlooking the Inner Harbour of Victoria.

German fresco painters decorated the ceilings and Italian stained glass was shipped to the site protected against breakage in layers of sweet molasses. Hand-painted tiles graced the fireplace and the highly polished hardwoods reflected the sunlight. An electric pump, a novelty for the time, circulated clear water through the fountain where songbirds splashed, and Mr. Pendray's spare time was spent mastering the art of garden topiary. He personally trained and clipped the yew, cedar, and holly bushes in the yard into a fantasy world of delightful animal shapes. His favorite was the huge teddy bear that held hidden Easter eggs for his enchanted children each spring.

A glimpse into the Pendray's enchanted life is available to you as a visitor for Afternoon Tea at the home he built for his family, now known as The Captain's Palace Inn. Whether you take your tea on the veranda or in the mansion, this delight should not be missed on your next visit to Victoria.

At the Captain's Palace tea is served daily from 2:00 p.m. to 4:00 p.m.

Tea! Thou soft, sober, sage and venerable liquid . . .
Colley Cibber

COTTAGE TEA ROOM

100 - 12220 Second Avenue
Steveston Village
Richmond, B.C.
Phone (604) 241-1853

Cottage Tea Room

The south arm of the Fraser River forms a well-used harbor at historic Steveston Village. Seals spy back at tourists from the water and tourists spy at fishing boats docked at Fisherman's Wharf to off-load their catch. Sea gulls circle overhead hoping for dinner and making greedy noises. There is something to do in Steveston at every season of the year, with much of it revolving around this maritime activity. You can book a river tour at the dock, and in April and May special sea lion tours will give you a close look at these huge sea mammals. In the winter, the sound of the fog horn replaces the rousing street music of summer and forms a slightly melancholy counterpoint to browsing the quaint shops that cluster close to the docks.

One block north of all these nautical pursuits you can escape to Cottage Tea Room, an excellent break for a castaway from the dock-side scene. Well-lit and peaceful, this cozy little tea room is a tribute to the owner's fond childhood memories of Lake District tea rooms in England. A collection of crisp linen tea towels from many English towns and villages form a colorful montage on one wall and a massive antique hutch commands another. The tablecloths reflect the owner Margaret's love of nature in sepia-toned, lace-trimmed bird and flower themes. During good weather the outdoor courtyard holds two umbrella tables covered in bright tropical floral cloths.

The English Tea Set includes a chocolate, cookies, assorted finger sandwiches, a freshly made scone with Devon Cream and jam with your tea for a very reasonable price. The menu also extends to homemade soup, sandwiches, pies and pastries. Margaret has a wide variety of teas to complement the food, and invests a great deal of thought to the comfort of her guests. The service is with grace and attentiveness. Thus renewed, one can then really enjoy a dock-side stroll and gift shop crawl in this quaint and little known corner of British Columbia.

Cottage Tea Room is open daily from 10 a.m. to 5 p.m. in summer. Please call ahead for hours during winter months.

THE EMPRESS HOTEL

721 Government Street
Victoria, B.C.
Phone (604) 384-8111

In the beginning there was The Empress, and it was good.

For more than 80 years this bastion of old world dignity has kept a detached and imposing vigil over the heads of camera packing tourists and aspiring bagpipers on Victoria's Inner Harbour. Grand in the European chateau tradition, it is the quintessential teatime destination for those seeking an authentic Afternoon Tea served elegantly in luxuriant surroundings.

The oldest of Victoria's afternoon teas is served in the Tea Lobby year-round with additional sittings in the Palm Court and Bengal Lounge during the summer season. Reservations should be made in advance, and attention should be given to "appropriate attire" to save embarrassment since T-shirts, shorts, jeans, and sweatsuits will have you turned away at the door.

Tea is served from sterling tea pieces and bone china. No detail is too small for the Empress to have perfected it. Decidedly formal yet comfortable in its setting, the tea includes fresh seasonal fruits, toasted honey crumpets, raisin scones with Jersey cream and fresh strawberry preserves, assorted tea sandwiches verging on art, pastries and the Empress Blend Tea. Ample enough to replace a meal or to carry you through to a fashionably late dinner, this is one of the pricier teas in the Northwest, $25 during summer of 1996, but tea at the Empress will continue to be an event you will remember.

Summer sittings in the Tea Lobby are 12:30 p.m., 2:00, 3:30, and 5 p.m. with extra sittings added during the peak summer months. The Palm Court opens June 25 and has sittings at 1 p.m., 2:30 and 4 p.m. Winter sittings are 2:00 and 3:30 p.m.

. . . and so the act of drinking tea must be attended by beauty.
Francis Ross Carpenter

GAZEBO TEA GARDEN

5460 Old West Saanich Road
Victoria, B.C.
Phone (604) 479-7787

Halfway between Victoria and Butchart Gardens, on a meandering rural Vancouver Island lane, is Gazebo Tea Garden. Cushioned from the road by tall trees and shady landscaping, the Gazebo Tea Garden is something of a landmark, established more than 17 years ago. Recently acquired by Michael and Treva Wallber, who bring to it more than 30 years combined experience in creating truly special and dramatic events, the Gazebo is a peaceful pastoral setting for afternoon tea or casual country meals under a natural canopy of old trees and climbing vines.

In its newest incarnation, the Gazebo is now available for weddings, showers, corporate meetings and tour groups. Seating is provided at outdoor bistro tables in a spacious fountain courtyard, or on their large deck where you can watch the backyard songbirds. The blend of bubbling water and bird song is one of our favorite sounds and is guaranteed, like tea, to rejuvenate your spirit. In the evening, thousands of twinkly lights adorn the trees and add romance to the candle-lit setting.

This is a business that is evolving creatively under the new proprietors, so share your ideas for a special tea or event with Treva. Then relax and know that all elements of your event are in extremely talented hands.

Gazebo Tea Garden is open for tea daily 11 a.m. to 4 p.m. from Easter to October 1, then 11 a.m. to 4 p.m. Wednesday through Sunday through the winter. Call for details.

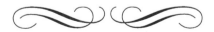

There is a great deal of poetry and fine sentiment in a chest of tea.
Ralph Waldo Emerson

Harp & Heather

9749 Willow Street
Chemainus, B.C.
Phone (604) 246-2434

Chemainus is a little town that rein-
vented itself and lays rightful claim to the
moniker "The little town that did."

Located on the eastern shoreline of
Vancouver Island, about an hour north of
Victoria with a view to Salt Spring Island,
Chemainus is one of the island's oldest
European settlements. In 1862 this farm-
ing community embraced the fledgling lumber industry by establishing a
small water-powered sawmill in its midst, and for the next 120 years the
production of high quality lumber defined Chemainus as a timber town. In
1983 the mill sputtered to a close after the single longest period of continuous
lumber production in western North America, leaving this community of
4,000 shaken economically and rethinking its identity.

Local businesspeople stepped forward with a vision for Chemainus. Their
plan, backed by British Columbia government financial help, would turn
Chemainus into Canada's largest permanent outdoor art gallery. Talented
muralists from around the globe travelled to Chemainus to capture the historical essence of the place and to translate it into colorful, giant illustrations
painted onto walls and buildings all over the little town. With 32 murals and
six sculptures now completed and many more planned, the spotlight of
worldwide media attention has resulted in a strong new renewable resource
industry for Chemainus, tourism. With more than 300,000 appreciative
visitors a year drinking in the visual history of this place, the indomitable
spirit of Chemainus has taken wing. Gift shops, inns, restaurants, antique
galleries, theater, and one notable tea room, Harp & Heather, dispense good
old fashioned hospitality.

Harp & Heather is located in an old building that, like the town, has
gone through several incarnations. Built as the town library, it later opened
its doors as the town's bank, and then a land management office. Charming
in detail and rich in history, the Afternoon Tea at Harp & Heather reflects
their Old World origins and are called the Welsh and Celtic Teas. It's a perfect
place to relax from strolling the outdoor mural art and marvelling in the
spirit of renewal of this charming little town. Call for details of special tea
events.

*Harp & Heather is usually open daily, 10:00 a.m. to 5:30 p.m., but best to call
ahead.*

JAMES BAY TEA ROOM

332 Menzies Street
Victoria. B.C.
Phone (604) 382-8282

Early on sleepy Sunday mornings in summer, the peace of the Inner Harbour of Victoria is roused by a goofy little water ballet performed by the seven diminutive harbor ferries. To strains of The Blue Danube waltz over a loudspeaker, the seven little passenger boats chug around the harbor forming a chorus line from which they peel off to carve watery figure eights, star bursts, and fleur de lis formations, weaving in and out of each other's wakes with the precision of water-bound Blue Angels. It's delightfully quirky to see these little water craft, which resemble Popeye's choice of cartoon transportation, performing intricate dock-side maneuvers with a serious looking captain at the wheel and often a sea gull riding along on the roof. It's part of the charm of the Inner Harbour and the silliness of the performance is what captivates and makes even the sleepy Sunday morning crowd begin the day with a smile.

The day begins early at James Bay Tea Room too, in the shadow of the dignified Parliament Buildings, a short walk from the harbor. Each day the doors open at 7:00 a.m. to greet early risers with a smile.

Touted as "An English Atmosphere in Victoria," this busy eatery operates from a charming old two-story, white clapboard house with cheerful striped awnings and hanging flower baskets. Inside the English country decor manifests itself in frilly curtains, chintz, copper tea kettles, and stained glass lamps lighting the dignified half-smiles of the jeweled and medalled Royal Family portraits lining the walls. Comfortable and unpretentious, like the English country cooking that owner Yvonne Woerpel champions, James Bay Tea Room has earned an excellent local reputation in its first ten years as the crowds will attest. Reservations are recommended, especially in summer. Sunday High Tea includes a rich English Trifle with the daily tea fare of sandwiches, tarts, cream scones and preserves.

It may be an English custom, but the James Bay Tea Room has perfected the ritual of Afternoon Tea, that most civilized of repasts. It is the perfect way to keep that silly ferry boat water ballet smile on your face through a pleasant Victoria afternoon.

James Bay Tea Room hours are 7:00 a.m. until 9:00 p.m. daily with Afternoon Tea served from 1:00 p.m. to 4:30 p.m..

Theme teas for your enjoyment!

MOTHER'S DAY TEA

Early in our marriage we invited Ken's ex-wife, Grace, to come stay for a few weeks' visit from her home in New Zealand. I liked her so much that strange thoughts like "What's wrong with that guy that he couldn't keep a marriage together with her," began to creep in (until I realized exactly how ludicrous that line of thinking was). I admire what a good mother Grace has been in raising Jenny and Mandy, both in their 30s now and trained professionals, but more importantly, kind and caring women. Mothering cannot be an easy job. All the more reason to honor them with their very own tea.

Decor

Roses and lace, all your prettiest things. (And be sure to wear clean underwear and stand up straight. You know how mothers are about those things.)

Music

Selections from the era that most of the mothers present first began their family, or classical.

Games

Ask each of the mothers to bring along three photos: one of their own mother, one of themselves as little girls, and one of their daughter. During the tea it is fun to play a game of trying to match up the mothers and daughters from a basket of photos. (Include some celebrity pictures from magazines too, like Debbie Reynolds-Carrie Fisher, Janet Leigh-Jamie Lee Curtis, Blythe Danner-Gwyneth Paltrow, you get the idea.)

Favors

A pretty pewter photo frame that will hold the photograph taken at the tea party.

HOTEL VANCOUVER

900 W. Georgia St., Vancouver, B.C. , Phone (604) 684-3131

The verdigris copper roof of the venerable Hotel Vancouver no longer dominates the skyline of Vancouver as it did long after it was built in 1939 by Canadian Pacific Railroad barons, but the cachet remains. Closed for remodelling until September or October 1996, the Hotel Vancouver is included here as a reminder to our readers and as a tribute to its prior position as the epicenter of afternoon tea culture in Vancouver for years. Call for specifics of their reopening for Afternoon Teas.

MURCHIE'S

Phone (604) 231-7500
Vancouver
970 Robson St.
City Square (12th & Cambie)
1030 West Georgia Street
Park Royal Mall (North)

Richmond
Richmond Centre (next to White Spot)

Burnaby	**White Rock**	**Victoria**
5000 Kingsway	**1959 - 152nd Street**	**1110 Government Street**

Murchie's is a tea retailer with a fine 100+ year tradition in the field. John Murchie, the founding father, was a tea blender and entrepreneur who delivered tea in his horse-drawn carriage. Scones are available to accompany the myriad blends.

"Take some more tea," The March Hare said to Alice very earnestly.
"I've had nothing yet," Alice replied in an offended tone,
"so I can't take more."
Lewis Carroll

OAK BAY BEACH HOTEL

1175 Beach Drive
Victoria, B.C.
Phone (604) 598-4556

I am married to an optimist who will pull me onto a bus and then find out where it's heading. With the same anticipation that Captain Vancouver must have felt turning the bow of his ship "Discovery" into the uncharted harbors of the island that bears his name, my husband is always certain there is some destination worthy of exploration on any city's community transit bus he picks at random. We have done this all over the world. Sometimes he's right. That was how we ventured out of downtown Victoria one beautiful summer day and found ourselves in the enchanting little community of Oak Bay.

Oak Bay hugs the shoreline of Haro Strait, the passage that separates Vancouver Island from the San Juan Islands of the U.S. fifteen miles to the east. Mount Baker forms a majestic backdrop to this maritime scene, and the fortunate visitor with sharp eyes may see the distinctive dorsal fins of resident orcas cruising the chilly waters. It is this breathtaking view that the 70-year-old Oak Bay Beach Hotel proudly overlooks, a dignified dowager separated from the natural shoreline by well-manicured grounds and pristine flower beds. The Oak Bay Beach Hotel has the old world charm of an English country gentleman's estate. The half-timbered Tudor styling seems in perfect harmony with their reputation for "Olde English comforts and fine service."

Inside, the serenity of dark wood mouldings and traditional appointments imbue the dining room with a stately and tranquil air. Afternoon Tea is held here in the casually elegant dining room, Bentley's on the Bay, from 2:30 to 5:00 p.m. daily. Manager Suzanne Dobie provides an open menu offering crumpets or scones with Devon cream, petite sandwiches, assorted pastries made by Chef Graham Plews, or a rich Sherry-laced trifle. A sampling of all of these treats is offered in the Traditional High Tea in case you cannot decide, or want a little heartier meal. In addition to excellent tea, a wide range of Sherry and Port are available.

No dress code is enforced here, but good taste abounds. The service is affable and efficient, and the staff will share some delightful ideas of what not to miss on your visit to Victoria. They can even arrange a whale-watching expedition for you on the hotel's own yacht or area tours in the summer on the Oak Bay Explorer, a double-decker sight-seeing bus. It's a wonderful neighborhood for a stroll along the waterfront or through quaint specialty shops as well.

The Oak Bay Beach Hotel dining Room, Bentley's on the Bay is open for tea from 2:30 to 5:00 p.m. daily.

Tea and Khaki for the British Raj in India

I think it was Napoleon who coined the phrase "An army marches on its stomach" and for the British army you'd better make sure that there's a cup of strong sweet tea to go with the food. It's even been said that we've put wars on hold while we "brewed up" our tea.

But in India in the 19th century one inspired army officer found another use for tea besides drinking it. Realizing that the traditional red tunics were too heavy and warm in the Indian summers most of the men wore white duck jackets and trousers. However both the red and the white tunics made excellent targets for the eagle-eyed, enemy riflemen. So the officer had his men brew up vats of tea and use it to dye their uniforms to a dull brown or tan, almost matching the dusty brown landscape. This became known as karkee and later officially as khaki drab. "Khak" being the Hindustani word for dust.

OLDE ENGLAND INN

**429 Lampson Street
Victoria, B.C.
Phone (604) 388-4353**

There is an interesting Yorkshire connection with a certain house in Victoria.

In 1910 a Yorkshire born investor, Thomas Slater, brought craftsmen over from England and Scotland to build his dream home, Rosmead. Built on a bluff overlooking the Strait of Juan de Fuca, and shielded from the road by tall Douglas firs, Rosmead was a rich example of half-timbered styling on a 5-acre estate. It changed hands several times over the next 20 years, and then in 1946 another Yorkshire couple, Sam and Rosina Lane, flew over from England intent on locating a mansion they could transform into an inn. They rediscovered Rosmead.

"From the start," Mrs. Lane explained, "our idea was to create a real English village of the Elizabethan period and we have now completed a number of replicas of famous places which are being added to the hotel."

They began with the birthplace of William Shakespeare and Anne Hathaway's Cottage. With a determination to maintain historical accuracy that included three years of exhaustive research, the Lanes tested the limits of endurance with the thatching of the roof of Anne Hathaway's Cottage. Through mildew and mice infestation they were able to nurse their thirteen acres of wheat to health and then flew an English thatcher in for the project.

Acquisition of a remarkable collection of period antiques occupied the free time of the Lane family, and many are displayed in the richly panelled Baronial Hall. A 300-year-old table once owned by the Bronte sisters may hold your tea service. Today Rosmead is known as Olde England Inn. It was named after Olde England Hotel on the shores of Lake Windemere in the English Lake District, and in the same spirit of hospitality, it offers unique rooms resplendent with antique furniture and period atmosphere. In the

Kings Rooms, for example, you will sleep in canopied royal beds where European crowned heads once rested (or tossed and turned depending on the state of the monarchy.)

Old Country Teas are offered Monday through Saturday, noon to 4:30 p.m. and on Sundays from 2 p.m. A full service restaurant offers meals served by a liveried staff of Elizabethan garbed "serviteurs and scullions." The Christmas feast here is legendary and an English Bobbie is on hand to direct traffic during the summer season and add to the English atmosphere.

What is the Yorkshire connection now? The menu indicates that the house Yorkshire pudding is from a 150-year-old recipe. Lose yourself in history and relax over tea exactly as they did in olde England.

Hours for tea are Monday through Saturday, noon to 4:30 p.m., and Sunday, 2:00 to 4:30 p.m.

Stands the church clock at ten to three?
And is there honey still for tea?
Rupert Brooke
The Old Vicarage

Point Ellice House

2616 Pleasant Street
Victoria, B.C.
Phone (604) 385-1518

When the cry of "Gold!" echoed along the canyons of the Fraser River in 1858, Victoria was transformed almost overnight from a quiet outpost for the Hudson Bay Company to the major outfitting head-quarters for the goldfields. The price of building lots in Victoria rose from $5 to $500 as more than 20,000 fortune hunters camped around the town. Thousands more arrived from Europe flushed with the prospects of easy wealth. One of these emigrants was Peter O'Reilly.

The Honourable Peter O'Reilly was born in England, but was raised and educated in Ireland where he rose through the ranks of the Irish Constabulary. In 1859 he rushed to British Columbia to seek his fortune and was appointed Gold Commissioner. While his life from then on was devoted to the causes of public service he was also active as a private investor in land and mining ventures, and became well entrenched in the social life of Victoria's upper middle class.

During the latter half of the nineteenth century the waterfront areas that became fashionable places to live were known as Victoria Arm and Selkirk Water. Large homes were built by prominent families on both sides of this harbor. Late in 1866 Peter O'Reilly and his pregnant wife Caroline purchased Point Ellice in order that their daughter Kathleen could be born there on the eve of the New Year 1867. Kathleen's life and the story of Point Ellice House become so intricately interwoven, that it would be impossible to separate the two. There are many to this day that feel Kathleen's spiritual presence is still attached to Point Ellice House, her home for all 78 years of her life.

Kathleen enjoyed all the privileges of upper middle class British Columbia. The lovely Italianate home and waterfront gardens were the site of much of the province's social life, and numerous opportunities arose for the petite and pretty Kathleen to select a suitor. But since the selection of a life-time mate would entail leaving her beloved Point Ellice home, Kathleen stalled and delayed the courting process until all such opportunities had passed. Decades ticked away and hearts were broken and mended, still Kathleen O'Reilly dwelled where her heart remained, among the gardens on the shores of Victoria Arm.

Today B.C. Heritage Attractions manages the property and conducts Afternoon Teas on the croquet lawn May 13 through September 8. A tape-recorded self-tour of the house and garden is the perfect introduction to tea.

All the furniture, art, wallpaper, china, clothing, ornaments, and even receipts are still as they were when Kathleen lived here. (See if you aren't aware of her presence as you pass the padded door that separates the servants' quarters from the main house and then again in the dining room.) The tea on the lawn includes fresh fruit, finger sandwiches, cream scones, fruit tart, short bread and lemon poppyseed cake. Evening and special events can be arranged, and a Fairy Tea in the garden for children is one of the popular seasonal activities.

As it was in the late 1800s, Point Ellice House has once again become a magnet for pleasant social activity and teas. Kathleen O'Reilly must be smiling again.

Tea at Point Ellice House is served outdoors on the croquet lawn May 13 through September 8, noon to 4:00 p.m.

With tea amuses the evening,
With tea solaces the midnight,
With tea welcomes the morning.
Samuel Johnson

RATTENBURY'S AT THE CRYSTAL GARDEN

700 block of Douglas Street
Victoria, B.C.
Phone (604) 381-1277
or 381-1213 recorded

In 1925, renowned Victoria architect Francis Rattenbury oversaw the creation of the largest saltwater swimming pool in the entire British Empire. The soaring glass roof, built in the European conservatory style, protected the bathers from the often inclement weather of winter Victoria, and provided shelter for such indulgent diversions as grand ballrooms, tea rooms and the promenade tropical conservatory the facility originally housed. It was one more jewel in the Inner Harbour architectural crown of Victoria, and survives to this day as The Crystal Garden adjacent to the Empress Hotel..

Still renowned for its expanded indoor tropical garden, the function of the building has evolved to reflect more selfless pursuits than saltwater frolics. Today's visitors are invited to explore a lush tropical habitat housing some 65 endangered species of birds, animals and vibrantly colored free-flying butterflies. Active in a wide variety of breeding and conservation programs, the Crystal Garden has taken on an ambitious project aimed at the reintroduction of some endangered species to their natural habitats. The efficacy of the project can be measured in terms of the breeding success of the Garden's two pairs of hyacinth macaws, which have parented eight noisy young, and the proliferation of the world's smallest (finger size) monkey, the pygmy marmoset's family to include twelve tiny yet robust babies.

Strolling amid preening flamingos and orchid blossoms can require sustenance, and the tradition of offering tea to visitors has proliferated from its origins here in the 1920s. Tea can be taken in the tropical splendor of the Crystal Garden daily from noon to 5:00 p.m. or next door at the full service Rattenbury's Restaurant. Both teas offer a full variety of finger sandwiches, scones, and sweets, and are an excellent way to spend a gray, misty afternoon in Victoria.

Hours for tea are noon to 5:00 p.m. daily, but call to confirm as changes may be planned.

ROYAL SCOT INN

425 Quebec Street
Victoria, B.C.
Phone (604) 388-5463

It was a Scotsman, James Douglas, who was commissioned in 1843 by the Hudson Bay Company to establish a fort in Victoria for the British. He rhapsodized about the area at the southern tip of Vancouver Island as "the most picturesque and decidedly most valuable part of the island that we had the good fortune to discover."

It was another Scotsman, John Blair, whose thoughtful design of Beacon Hill Park 45 years later, would begin the era for Victoria as the "City of Gardens", and whose layout and plant recommendations, as evidenced by the hybrid rhododendrons planted around Fountain Lake, have thrived for the past 100 years. Victoria has a lot to thank Scotland for.

One block west of the imposing Parliament Buildings is Victoria's Suite Hotel, The Royal Scot. The Royal Scot is home to Jonathan's Restaurant where Afternoon Tea is served daily and their open menu includes your own selection, rather than a preset assortment, of scones, bagels, sandwiches, toast, pies and fruit plates as well as a broad selection of ports and sherries served in a coffee shop setting or at outdoor tables in a small courtyard.

Jonathan's Afternoon Teas at The Royal Scot are served from 2:30 p.m. to 5:00 p.m.

They are at the end of the gallery;
Retired to their tea and scandal.
William Congreve

SECRET GARDEN TEA COMPANY

5559 West Boulevard
Vancouver, B.C.
Phone (604) 261-3070

The fashionably eclectic neighborhood of Kerrisdale in Vancouver has a secret that you are invited to share. You are personally invited to take a few moments from your normally busy life and enter the door of the Secret Garden "where the traditions of afternoon tea are delightfully intertwined with the comforts of home."

High tea is served daily with formal tea service, fine English antique china, and fresh flowers and ivy on the three-tiered serving tray from 2:30 to 4:30 p.m. or a mini tea served between 1:00 and 5:00 p.m. (Someone privy to this secret simply cannot be trusted, since it is so busy for teatime that you must make reservations 24 hours in advance now. We're sure we can trust you though, you have such an honest face.)

The room is comfortable and charming with a soft sofa that rises around you like a soft embrace and a large welcoming fireplace hearth topped with a bouquet laden mantel. Bright, homey accent pieces (many for sale) please the eye everywhere you gaze, and the selection of over 100 teas is sure to please the pickiest palate. It's like being invited to a friend's lovely home for tea, without the nagging obligatory feeling that you should volunteer to help her clean up afterwards. Go ahead, get comfy, food this tasty deserves to be savored.

Located in an area that is giving birth to interesting shopping and strolling opportunities, The Secret Garden owners Kathy Wyder and Andrea Wadman take delight in creating a special afternoon tea for you using "no mixes or artificial ingredients" whatsoever. Available for special events, showers, anniversaries and birthdays, you really should indulge yourself on occasion. Face it, you're becoming your mother anyway, so why don't you let her in on this secret? She has such an honest face.

Open daily from 1:00 p.m. to 5:00 p.m. (see above for details).

THE SUTTON PLACE HOTEL

845 Burrard Street
Vancouver, B.C.
Phone (604) 682-5513

The Salish Indians have long seen the beauty and plenty in the area the Europeans called Vancouver. With the backdrop of dramatic mountains, they resided in peace for a couple thousand years on land that rose 38 feet above the pristine saltwater inlets and bays. The abundant land provided all they required for shelter, and food was varied and plentiful.

The first European settlers arrived a little over 130 years ago, and perhaps inspired by the plank houses the Salish built, constructed the first sawmill. Census reports show that the settlement had grown to only 2,000 inhabitants twenty years after the mill was built, but that was soon to change. From the mountains to the east, the rythmic sound of metal ringing on metal could be heard in 1886 as the final miles of track were laid for the transcontinental railroad that would forever change Vancouver. Within a couple of years the population had swelled to 27,000 as Vancouver became the western railroad terminus.

Today Vancouver has blossomed into a metropolitan area that is home to 1.5 million people, which is more than half of the entire population of British Columbia. It is the third largest city in Canada, and the fastest growing metropolitan area in North America. Enlightened urban planning has resulted in a municipality of 135 parks covering some 2,700 acres. Since no major urban freeway cuts and scars the city, you are forced to slow down, exactly like you must do to enjoy a good Afternoon Tea.

Afternoon Tea is offered at The Sutton Place Hotel (formerly Le Meridien) in the heart of the city, just a block away from popular and trendy Robson Street boutiques and eateries. (Robson Street becomes Robson Strasse west of Burrard Street which speaks to the European influence in this retail area.) Teatime at Cafe Fleuri, located in the hotel and orchestrated by Patricia Clairmont, is a soothing and tranquil experience, lightyears away from the frenzied energy of Robson. It is an excellent place to relax from sightseeing or shopping or to simply unwind between 2:30 and 5:00 p.m., Monday through Saturday.

Reminiscent of stately European manors, the hotel is furnished with period antiques, crystal chandeliers, and opulent floral displays; all the lovely Old World appeal and comfort of a fine home. A subdued elegance, without a hint of stuffiness, permeates the tea time here. From the softness of peach-toned plush wall covering and glossy white wainscoting to floral-print skirted tables, the decor inspires lingering in the casual informality. Afternoon tea here is abundant, and begins with of an array of the tastiest of English finger sandwiches, artfully presented. French pastries and the richest of warm

TeaTime in the Northwest

scones served with local berry jams and Devonshire cream follow. You choose your tea from 11 different and widely varying types which include their delicious house blend, a perfect complement to their scones - the Sutton Afternoon Blend. The service is attentive without encroaching on the most private of tea time conversation. The hotel is a favorite of well-travelled celebrities. This comes as no surprise when you view all the attention to detail and tasteful touches that Sutton Place puts into their hospitality.

As a thoughtful tribute to the rapidly-growing Asian community in Vancouver, they also offer what they call a Sutton Style Japanese Tea Ceremony, a synthesis of east and west, with a selection of three different, high quality Green Teas.

Once again, as 130 years ago, you can indulge in the abundance of Vancouver and rest assured that all your needs will be met and exceeded in the nicest possible way.

Tea is served 2:30 to 5:30 p.m., Monday through Saturday.

I suppose no person ever enjoyed with more relish
the infusion of this fragrant leaf than did Johnson.
James Boswell

THE TEA ROOM AT PLAZA ESCADA

757 West Hastings Street
Sinclair Centre
Vancouver, B.C.
Phone (604) 688-8558

Everything about the Tea Room at Plaza Escada is Euro design-conscious, youthful, freshly modern, and pulsing with an upbeat attitude. It is, therefore, exactly what you would expect from an elite ladies fashion boutique catering to smart, self-reliant, youthful, vigorous working women of exceptionally high levels of both style and disposable income.

In keeping with the less-is-more theory, the setting at Plaza Escada's tearoom is sleek and uncluttered without being sterile. There is a no-nonsense approach to tea featuring the Republic of Tea's complete array. Since there really is no traditional Afternoon Tea here, you're free to have it anytime you want, 10:00 a.m. to closing at 6:00 p.m., Monday through Saturday. The experience is altogether refreshing. More than 40 types of tea are offered, and you can nibble delectable biscotti.

Immerse yourself in something new, imaginative and creative. Have tea at the Tea Room at Plaza Escada next time you're in downtown Vancouver.

Tea is served from 10:00 a.m. to 6:00 p.m., Monday through Saturday.

Tea is drunk to forget the din of the world.
T'ien Yiheng

Windsor House Tea Room

2540 Windsor Road
Victoria, B.C.
Phone (604) 595-3135

Locals jest that a visit to Oak Bay is so British it's like crossing behind "the Tweed Curtain." It's true that this spectacular little community unabashedly revels in its authentically British roots, after all, reminders of them abound. Even Rudyard Kipling felt at home here. While riding the free double decker bus you pass by Tudor-style shopping areas, tea rooms, crisp white cricket matches, and lovingly nurtured rose gardens. Steak and kidney pie aromas emanate from kitchen windows. Tweed-jacketed men with canes walk behind well-mannered Welsh Corgis and Jack Russells to the local pub. Cultured civility extends even to that dying art form, courteous driving.

A welcoming two story Tudor style building a block from the rocky shoreline of Oak Bay has been home to the Windsor House Tea Room for only the past five years. The air of British Empire permanence and stability it emanates bespeaks decades longer. Great taste and care have gone into the refurbishing of this old dwelling, from authentic Victorian floral patterned wallpaper and coved ceilings to the simplicity of the blue and white china service. An attractive array of gift items adorn and tempt at the same time. Lace curtains filter the sunlight through mullioned windows, and the hardwoods are polished and bright.

Their "Traditional High Tea" is offered daily from 2:30 to 5:00 p.m. as well as homemade soups, salads, and meat pies. The menu says "A good meal...a good friend...a time treasured," and the Windsor House Tea Room is a delightful place to while away an afternoon in charming surroundings.

Tea is offered everyday, 2:30 to 5:30 p.m.

FAVORITE TEA TIME RECIPES

SANDWICHES & SAVORIES

TOMATO-BASIL TEA SANDWICHES

So simple and such a nice blend of fresh flavors we are indebted to our friend, Tom Caulton, for this tea sandwich and much more. Inventor, composer, computer genius, Tom is one of those people that occupies a higher mental plane than just about anyone we know.

8   slices white bread
1/2   cup ricotta cheese
    Salt and pepper
1   T. your choice of Italian salad dressing
2   small ripe tomatoes, sliced
8   fresh basil leaves

Cut a circle of bread from each slice, using a round cookie cutter. Mix the ricotta cheese with salt and pepper to taste and 1 T. Italian salad dresing. Place a tomato slice on each of the four rounds, top with a basil leaf and cover with remaining round. Cut in half to yield 16 tea sandwiches.

Nutritional Analysis per Serving
Calories: 54, Total Fat: 1.9 g., Saturated Fat: .8 g.
Cholesterol: 4 mg., Carbohydrate: 7.2 g., Dietary Fiber: .5 g.
Protein: 2.0 g., Sodium: 82 mg.

PEAR AND STILTON SANDWICHES

The last day of one trip to England found us in Winchester on a chilly autumn day. Sitting by a fire in a tearoom with Pear and Stilton Sandwiches, a glass of Port, and a pot of tea refreshed us for our usual mad dash to the airport for the return flight home.

4   very thin slices honey-oat bread
1   T. butter, softened
1   ripe pear, Bosc or Anjou, halved
    and thinly sliced
    fresh lemon juice
2   T. crumbled Stilton cheese (about 1/2 oz.)

Spread each slice of bread with the softened butter. Sprinkle the pear slices with lemon juice. Place half of the pear slices in a single layer on a slice of bread. Top with half of the crumbled cheese and a second bread slice. Repeat, using the remaining pear, cheese and bread. Trim crusts and cut into 8 finger sandwiches.

Nutritional Analysis per Serving
Calories: 68, Total Fat: 2.6 g., Saturated Fat: 1.3 g.
Cholesterol: 5 mg., Carbohydrate: 9.9 g., Dietary Fiber: 1.0 g.
Protein: 1.6 g., Sodium: 120 mg.

CUCUMBER TEA SANDWICHES

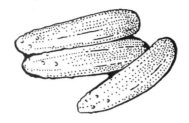

Samuel Johnson said, "A cucumber should be well sliced, and dressed with pepper and vinegar, and then thrown out, as good for nothing." My husband agrees with him, but I do not.

2	medium cucumbers, peeled, sliced thin
1	cup apple cider vinegar
1	T. sugar
	salt and pepper
	Fresh mint leaves
1/4	cup mayonnaise

Marinate the cucumber slices in the brine made from the vinegar, sugar, salt and pepper for at least an hour. Drain well. Remove the crusts from 6 slices of thin white bread. Spread lightly with mayonnaise. Lay four fresh mint leaves on each of 3 slices. Over the top of the mint leaves layer the drained cucumber slices. Top with the other bread slice, mayonnaise side down, and cut into four small finger sandwiches. Garnish with mint. Makes 12 tea sandwiches.

Nutritional Analysis per Serving
Calories: 77, Total Fat: 4.2 g., Saturated Fat: .7 g.
Cholesterol: 3 mg., Carbohydrate: 9 g., Dietary Fiber: .7 g.
Protein: 1.4 g., Sodium: 117 mg.

CUCUMBER HERB BUTTER TEA SANDWICHES

Sir Compton McKenzie (1883-1972), in describing an English tea party, was not very charitable to the cucumber. Since I love cucumbers, I detest this quote. Ken, however, detests cucumbers and finds it fitting: "You are offered a piece of bread and butter that feels like a damp handkerchief and sometimes, when cucumber is added to it, like a wet one."

1	medium cucumber, peeled and salted to taste
4	T. butter, softened
1/2	T. fresh dill
4	thin slices of firm white bread, crusts removed

Cut the cucumber into thin slices and place them on a paper towel. Salt the cucumber lightly and cover with a paper towel. Let stand for a half hour so that any extra moisture is absorbed.

In a blender or a bowl, combine the butter and the chopped dill. Lightly spread the butter on each slice of bread, buttering all the way to the edges.

Place 9 or more cucumber slices on one slice of bread, layering them in three rows. Top with a second slice of bread. Cut the sandwich with a sharp, serrated knife diagonally to create triangles. Makes 8 finger sandwiches.

Nutritional Analysis per Serving
Calories: 89, Total Fat: 6.2 g., Saturated Fat: 3.6 g.
Cholesterol: 15 mg., Carbohydrate: 7.3 g., Dietary Fiber: .6 g.
Protein: 1.4 g., Sodium: 126 mg.

CARMELIZED WALLA WALLA SWEET AND CREAM CHEESE TEA SANDWICH

1	Walla Walla Sweet onion, finely chopped
3	tsp. butter
4	slices of raisin bread
1/4	cup cream cheese

Heat butter in skillet over medium-low heat. Add onion and cook, stirring often, about 15 to 20 minutes, until the onion is brown and carmelized. Remove from heat and allow to cool.

Spread cream cheese over bread. Spread onions over two of the slices and top with the other two slices.

Wrap and refrigerate until firm, about 15 minutes. Trim crusts, cut into four rectangles. Makes 8 tea sandwiches.

Nutritional Analysis per Serving
Calories: 77, Total Fat: 4.4 g., Saturated Fat: 2.5 g.
Cholesterol: 12 mg., Carbohydrate: 7.7 g., Dietary Fiber: .8 g.
Protein: 1.9 g., Sodium: 106 mg.

Dungeness Crab and Black Olive Tea Sandwiches

8 oz. softened cream cheese
1/4 lb. Dungeness crabmeat
1/2 cup chopped black olives, drained
1 medium cucumber, peeled and sliced into 20 very thin slices
1 bunch fresh watercress sprigs
1 T. lemon peel
1 French baguette, sliced thin.

Beat the cream cheese until smooth, blend in the crab and olives until well mixed. Spread 1 tablespoon crab mixture onto each slice of French bread and top with cucumber slices and sprig of watercress. Top with remaining thinly sliced baguette to form a sandwich.

Makes 20 finger sandwiches.

Nutritional Analysis per Serving
Calories: 113, Total Fat: 5.1 g., Saturated Fat: 2.7 g.
Cholesterol: 17 mg., Carbohydrate: 12.8 g., Dietary Fiber: .8 g.
Protein: 4.1 g., Sodium: 219 mg.

WATERCRESS, RADISH AND CREAM CHEESE TEA SANDWICHES

1   bunch radishes (about 8 small radishes)
2   thin slices 5 grain bread
4   tsp. cream cheese
6   sprigs watercress (leaves only, no stems)
    salt to taste

Wash and cut the radishes into very thin slices. Spread the cream cheese on the bread. Press 3 sprigs of watercress into the cream cheese on each slice of bread. Top each with a few slices of radish and salt lightly. Cut each slice into 4 finger sandwiches. Serve open-faced. Makes 8 tea sandwiches.

Nutritional Analysis per Serving
Calories: 27, Total Fat: 1.1 g., Saturated Fat: .6 g.
Cholesterol: 3 mg., Carbohydrate: 3.5 g., Dietary Fiber: .4 g.
Protein: .8 g., Sodium: 83 mg.

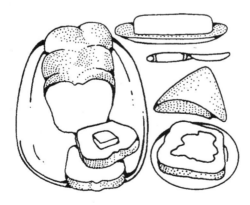

CHICKEN ALMOND FINGER SANDWICHES

Shelley's Spot of Tea • Tacoma, Washington

- 2 freshly cooked breasts or1 can all white chicken
- 1/2 cup finely crushed almonds
- 1/3 cup mayonnaise
  - hazelnut bread
  - green grapes

Mix chopped chicken with almonds and mayonaisse. Spread bread with light layer of cream cheese. Add a light layer of the chicken salad. Slice very fine 3 to 4 grapes, layer on top. Cut crusts from bread. Cut into 4 long fingers.

Top with dot of cream cheese, a small piece of grape and a sliver of almond.

Serve with a cluster of grapes on the side. Makes 8 finger sandwiches.

Nutritional Analysis per Serving
Calories: 232, Total Fat: 16.6 g., Saturated Fat: 2.8 g.
Cholesterol: 34 mg., Carbohydrate: 9.1 g., Dietary Fiber: 1.3 g.
Protein: 12.4 g., Sodium: 149 mg.

MINI-SHRIMP SANDWICHES

Along the Oregon coast you can get shrimp so fresh and tasty that you can find yourself trying to work them into every recipe. Here's one way to make room for them on your tea table.

8	oz. whipped cream cheese
8	oz. salad shrimp, diced
1	clove garlic
1/4	cup chopped chives
1/4	tsp. salt
	Freshly ground pepper
1	stick butter
	Juice of 1 small lemon
2	tsp. fresh parsley
20	slices thinly sliced white bread

Mix together cream cheese, shrimp, garlic, chives, salt and pepper. In a separate bowl, cream butter, adding lemon juice and parsley. Spread butter mixture on 10 slices bread, then spread on the cream cheese/shrimp mixture.

Top with the remaining bread slices and remove crusts. Cut each sandwich into 4 triangles or 4 squares.

Makes 40 tea sandwiches.

Nutritional Analysis per Serving
Calories: 80, Total Fat: 4.8 g., Saturated Fat: 2.8 g.
Cholesterol: 21 mg., Carbohydrate: 6.5 g., Dietary Fiber: .3 g.
Protein: 2.7 g., Sodium: 129 mg.

EAST INDIAN TEA SANDWICHES

*When India was part of the British Empire, afternoon tea
was introduced there. This recipe shows the successful
blending of those cultures.*

3/4	cup chopped cooked chicken breast
1/3	cup chutney
1/4	tsp. curry powder
2/3	cup mayonaisse
6	slices bread

Mix together and spread 3 tablespoons on each slice of
bread. Trim crusts and cut into 4 equal strips.

Nutritional Analysis per Serving
Calories: 80, Total Fat: 5.8 g., Saturated Fat: 1.0 g.
Cholesterol: 8 mg., Carbohydrate: 5.0 g., Dietary Fiber: .3 g.
Protein: 2.2 g., Sodium: 83 mg.

CRAB AND HERB MINI PASTIE

Tea and Tomes • Newport, Oregon

*The wonderful fresh crab, abundant in our waters makes this recipe
from Newport's newest and best tea room especially tasty.*

8   oz. herbed cream cheese (make it yourself
     or buy it at the grocers)
1/4 lb. fresh or frozen crab meat, thoroughly drained
1/4 cup black olives, drained and chopped
1   T coarsely shredded lemon peel

2   sheets puff pastry dough - thawed

Mix together the cream cheese, crab, olives and lemon
peel - set aside. Using a 2 in. round cookie cutter, cut 24
rounds from pastry. Place 1 tsp. crab filling on each
round, fold over into half circle.

Using a fork crimp edges to seal. Place on an ungreased
baking sheet and bake for 15min at 350 or until golden
brown. Serve warm with or without dusting of parsley
over top.

Makes 24 mini pasties.

*Nutritional Analysis per Serving
Calories: 168, Total Fat: 12.5 g., Saturated Fat: 3.4 g.
Cholesterol: 14 mg., Carbohydrate: 11 g., Dietary Fiber: 0 g.
Protein: 3.3 g., Sodium: 113 mg.*

GARDEN PEAS AND SHRIMP ON TOAST

We've given up trying to grow peas. The rabbits find them irresistable. Fortunately good farmers' markets abound in our area.

1 stick butter, softened
1/4 lb. shelled fresh peas, rinsed
    Salt and pepper to taste
1 clove fresh garlic, minced
1/4 lb. fresh salad shrimp
8 oz. softened cream cheese
4 slices toasted bread, crusts removed
1 tsp. finely chopped dill
1 tsp. thyme

Melt 2 tablespoons butter in medium skillet. Add the peas and saute gently for about 8 minutes. Season to taste with salt and pepper, remove from heat. Allow to cool.

After the peas have cooled, add 4 tablespoons butter, garlic, and shrimp. Spread the toast with the remaining butter, the cream cheese, and top with the pea-shrimp mixture. Sprinkle with dill and thyme.

Cut into four squares or triangles. Serves 4.

Nutritional Analysis per Serving
Calories: 522, Total Fat: 44.2 g., Saturated Fat: 27.1 g.
Cholesterol: 180 mg., Carbohydrate: 18.6 g., Dietary Fiber: 2.1 g.
Protein: 14.2 g., Sodium: 602 mg.

CRAB-FILLED PUFFS

While living in Alaska for eight years, I learned to use crab in many recipes. Here is one that is a suitable and festive addition to your tea.

Crab filling:
1	lb. crabmeat, flaked
4	hard-boiled eggs, finely chopped
1/4	cup celery, finely chopped
1/4	cup onion, finely chopped
1	T. fresh parsley, minced
2	T. chili sauce
1-1/2	cup mayonnaise
	salt and pepper to taste

Mix all ingredients together, adding enough mayonnaise to bind. Refrigerate until shortly before serving. Fill puffs immediately prior to serving.

Puffs:
1	cup water
1/2	cup butter
1	cup sifted flour
4	eggs

Bring water to boiling, add butter. Stir until melted. Add flour, stirring briskly until dough forms a ball. Beat eggs until very thick and lemony-colored. Stir into cooled dough; blend thoroughly. Drop by teaspoonfuls onto baking sheet. Bake in preheated 400° F. oven for 15 minutes. Cool on rack.

To serve, slice and fill immediately prior to serving. Makes 24 puffs.

Nutritional Analysis per Serving
Calories: 194, Total Fat: 16.7 g., Saturated Fat: 4.6 g.
Cholesterol: 104 mg., Carbohydrate: 4.8 g., Dietary Fiber: .1 g.
Protein: 6.3 g., Sodium: 224 mg.

CHICKEN SALAD

Attic Secrets • Marysville, Washington

"And we meet, with champagne and a chicken, at last."
Lady Mary Wortley Montague
"The Lover"

4	cooked chicken breasts (boneless and skinless)
1/2	cup mayonaisse
1/4	cup chopped pecans
2	T. chopped celery
1/2	tsp. onion powder
	Salt and pepper to taste

Serve on lettuce or as a spread. Yields 6 servings.

Nutritional Analysis per Serving
Calories: 265, Total Fat: 18.8 g., Saturated Fat: 2.7 g.
Cholesterol: 65 mg., Carbohydrate: 1.6 g., Dietary Fiber: .4 g.
Protein: 22.1 g., Sodium: 212 mg.

CHIVE BLOSSOMS

Blossom by blossom
The spring begins.
Algernon C. Swinburne

1 box frozen puff pastry sheets
  (2 sheets) thawed
1 8 oz. container soft cream cheese
  with chives spread
  Garnishes: watercress or parsley

Bring cream cheese to room temperature. Preheat oven to 375° F. Unfold pastry and place on lightly floured surface. Roll lightly to eliminate fold lines.

Using a 2-1/2" scalloped cookie cutter, cut about 18 circles from each sheet. Gently press the pastry circles into ungreased cups of miniature muffin pans. Pastry will resemble a flower.

Fill each lined cup with about 1/2 tsp. cream cheese and bake 15 to 20 minutes. Cool slightly, remove from pan onto wire rack and top each with sprig of watercress or parsley. Makes 36.

Serve warm.

Nutritional Analysis per Serving
Calories: 281, Total Fat: 20.1 g., Saturated Fat: 3.9 g.
Cholesterol: 7 mg., Carbohydrate: 21.4 g., Dietary Fiber: 0.0 g.
Protein: 3.9 g., Sodium: 136 mg.

SCOTCH EGGS

*I ate my very first Scotch Egg in Wales at a little pub in coastal Conwy.
I remember looking at it and thinking "How'd they do that?" Conwy
Castle, built in 1292, today houses Britain's first and most famous
teapot museum. Home to more than 1,000 pots, there is also a gift
shop called Char Bazaar for replicas.*

2 tsp. all-purpose flour
4 hard boiled eggs, shelled
1 tsp. Worcestshire sauce
1/2 lb. bulk pork sausage
1 egg, beaten
1 cup fine dry bread crumbs
Vegetable oil for deep-frying
Parsley for garnish

Combine flour with salt and pepper in a small bowl,
sprinkle over eggs. Add the Worcestshire sauce to sausage and mix well. Divide sausage into 4 equal portions
and form each into a flat patty.

Place 1 of the hard boiled eggs into the center of each
patty and shape the meat around the egg, covering the
egg completely.

Coat the meat with the beaten egg, then roll in bread
crumbs. Heat 3 inches of oil to 350° F. and gently add the
meat-covered eggs. Cook for 7 or 8 minutes until crisp
and golden.

Drain on paper towels and cool before slicing in half and
serving, garnishing cut side with the fresh parsley.

Makes 8 halves. Serve with salad for high tea.

*Nutritional Analysis per Serving (One-half egg)
Calories: 253, Total Fat: 18.9 g., Saturated Fat: 5.7 g.
Cholesterol: 152 mg., Carbohydrate: 11.2 g., Dietary Fiber: .7 g.
Protein: 8.9 g., Sodium: 330 mg.*

SALMON MANICOTTI

Nutcracker Tea Room • Issaquah, Washington

UNIT 1.
14 1/2 OR 15 1/2 oz can of salmon.
2 cups small curd cottage cheese
2 eggs well beaten
1/2 cup minced onion
1/4 cup chopped parsley
1/2 tsp. dillweed
8-10 Manicotti shells, cooked and drained.

UNIT 2.
3 T. butter
3 T. flour
1 cup milk
2 cups jack cheese, grated
1/4 cup Parmesan cheese, grated

Drain and flake salmon, reserving liquid. Combine Unit 1 ingredients and fill shells.

Melt butter, add flour. Add milk to reserved salmon liquid to make 1-1/2 cups

Stir into flour paste to make white sauce. Stir in 1 cup of grated Jack cheese until melted.

Pour half the sauce into a baking dish and add stuffed shells. Cover with remaining sauce. Sprinkle with the other cup of grated Jack cheese and the 1/2 cup Parmesan cheese. Cover. Bake 10 minutes at 450° F.

Uncover. Bake 10 more minutes until bubbly. Serves 4.

Nutritional Analysis per Serving
Calories: 920, Total Fat: 41.1 g., Saturated Fat: 22 g.
Cholesterol: 255 mg., Carbohydrate: 68 g., Dietary Fiber: 2.3 g.
Protein: 66.9 g., Sodium: 1,647 mg.

WELSH RAREBIT

James Bay Tearoom • Victoria, B.C.

1/4	lb. margarine
3/4	cups flour
3	cups milk
3	oz. ale or flat beer
2	cups sharp Cheddar, grated
3	T. hot mustard
3	T. Worcestershire sauce.

Melt 1/4 lb. margarine over medium heat. Gradually add 3/4 cups of flour, blend with a whisk to form a roux.

Sitrring constantly, gradually add 3 cups of milk. Add 3 ozs. ale or flat beer, then add 2 cups grated sharp Cheddar. Stir in 3 T. hot mustard and 3 T. Worcestershire sauce.

Mix thoroughly and cook slowly over low heat stirring often. Cook until well blended.

Serve hot over toasted bread, muffins or crumpets with a green salad. Serves 6

Nutritional Analysis per Serving
Calories: 417, Total Fat: 30.7 g., Saturated Fat: 12.2 g.
Cholesterol: 51 mg., Carbohydrate: 20.4 g., Dietary Fiber: .25 g.
Protein: 14.4 g., Sodium: 612 mg.

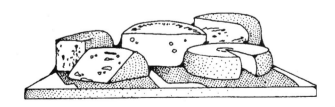

ORIENTAL TEA HONEY RIBS

        2   lb. pork spareribs
        1   cup strong brewed Lapsong Souchon tea
      1/4   cup soy sauce
      1/2   cup honey

Place ribs in baking pan, cover, bake 425° F. for 1 hour.
Pour off all fat, cut ribs into pieces. Combine tea with
other ingredients. Pour over ribs and bake, uncovered,
basting periodically for 30 or 40 more minutes (or until
crispy brown and tender.) Serves 4.

Nutritional Analysis per Serving
Calories: 786, Total Fat: 53.6 g., Saturated Fat: 20.3 g.
Cholesterol: 177 mg., Carbohydrate: 36.3 g., Dietary Fiber: .2 g.
Protein: 39.7 g., Sodium: 1,005 mg.

SCONES, BREADS & MUFFINS

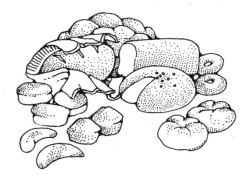

OATMEAL BREAKFAST SCONES

*Scones originated in Scotland near the town of Scone
which is known for much more than tea-time biscuits. For centuries
Scottish rulers were crowned while seated on a large, mystical
Coronation Stone, known as the "Stone of Scone." In 1296, the
conquering English army under Edward I confiscated the stone in
an effort to unify all Britain. Today the stone rests under the
Coronation throne in Westminister Abbey and is an important
component in the crowning of British monarchs.*

*Prepared correctly, this authentic scone recipe will not resemble the
Stone of Scone.*

1	cup all-purpose flour
1	cup rolled oats
1/2	tsp. baking soda
1/2	tsp. salt
1	tsp. cream of tartar
1	T. sugar
1/4	cup shortening
1/2	cup milk

Preheat oven to 425° F. Mix together flour, oats, baking
soda, salt, cream of tartar, and sugar. Add the shortening
and milk, and mix with fork into a soft dough. Roll out
on a floured board to 1/2 " thickness. Cut into triangles.
Place on greased baking sheet, and bake for 15 minutes
or until lightly browned. Serve for breakfast or tea, warm
with butter and jam. Makes 8-12 scones.

*Nutritional Analysis per Serving
Calories: 135, Total Fat: 6.2 g., Saturated Fat: 1.6 g.
Cholesterol: 2 mg., Carbohydrate: 17 g., Dietary Fiber: .9 g.
Protein: 3.0 g., Sodium: 70 mg.*

OAK BAY SCONES

Oak Bay Beach Hotel • Victoria, B.C.

Chef Graham Plews brought this recipe to the Oak Bay Beach Hotel in 1994 from his family recipe file.

1-1/2	lb. flour
8	oz. sugar
2	oz. baking powder
8	oz. shortening
4	eggs
1	cup buttermilk

Sift dry ingredients together. Cut in shortening to a fine crumb. Beat eggs and blend with milk. Combine wet and dry ingedients

Knead dough slightly to firm up for rolling. Roll dough to 3/4" thickness and cut into 3" rounds

Bake at 375 F. for 20-30 minutes. Makes 24 scones.

Nutritional Analysis per Serving
Calories: 241, Total Fat: 10.7 g., Saturated Fat: 2.7 g.
Cholesterol: 36 mg., Carbohydrate: 32.3 g., Dietary Fiber: 0 g.
Protein: 4.3 g., Sodium: 208 mg.

CANDIED GINGER SCONES

Butchart Gardens • Victoria, B.C.

5	cups all-purpose flour
2	tsp. baking powder
1/3	cup white sugar
1-1/4	cup unsalted butter
1/2	cup candied ginger
5	large eggs
2/3 + 2 Tsp	milk (2%)

Preheat oven to 350° F. Mix flour, baking powder and sugar together in a medium-sized bowl. Dice candied ginger. Using a pastry cutter, blend butter and candied ginger into flour mixture until butter is in pea sized pieces.

In a separate bowl, mix eggs and milk. Add milk mixture to flour/butter mixture and blend until combined. Place dough on a lightly floured counter and knead lightly.

Roll dough to a 1/2" thickness. Cut into 3" circles.

Place on an unfloured baking sheet and bake at 350° F. for 15 - 20 minutes, until golden brown. Makes 24.

Nutritional Analysis per Serving
Calories: 228, Total Fat: 11.7 g., Saturated Fat: 6.8 g.
Cholesterol: 76 mg., Carbohydrate: 23.2 g., Dietary Fiber: 0 g.
Protein: 4.4 g., Sodium: 49 mg.

TEA AN' TIQUES SCONES

Spokane, Washington

*Owner Jackie Hayes was given this recipe by a good friend,
and finds it versatile enough to change with addition of spices, fruits or
cheese. Here's your chance to get creative.*

    2   cups flour
    1   cup oats
    1/4 cup sugar (Omit if making a cheese
         or herb scone.)
    1   T. baking powder
    1/2 tsp. salt
    1/4 tsp. cream of tarter
    1/2 cup butter
    1/3 cup buttermilk, cream or milk
    2   eggs
    1-1/2 tsp. vanilla (omit for a herb scone or
         substitute with extracts of almond,
         lemon, orange , etc.)

Combine dry ingredients and cut in butter using a pastry blender until mixture resembles coarse meal. Add remaining ingredients and blend well to form a dough.

Press into a round cake pan and bake at 425° F. for 15-18 minutes then cut into 8 wedges to serve.

Serve warm with jams, honey or a heated cream cheese for the herb or cheese scones.

Makes 8 scones.

Nutritional Analysis per Serving
Calories: 339, Total Fat: 14.4 g., Saturated Fat: 7.8 g.
Cholesterol: 84 mg., Carbohydrate: 44.2 g., Dietary Fiber: 0 g.
Protein: 8.5 g., Sodium: 413 mg.

TEA-THYME BISCUITS

*Thyme, fresh from your own herb garden, makes this
savory biscuit a treat and always reminds us of the bed and breakfast
in Wales where we first tasted these.*

4	cups flour
2	T. baking powder
1-1/2	tsp. salt
4	T. fresh thyme, chopped fine
1	cup butter
2	eggs
1	cup milk

Preheat oven to 450° F. Combine dry ingredients including the thyme. Cut the butter into them with a pastry
blender. Beat the eggs with the milk and add all at once
to the flour mixture. Mix just until combined. Drop
heaping tablespoons onto greased cookie sheet and bake
10-12 minutes. Makes 40 small biscuits. Our hostess
served these with sliced cheese and apple for a nice blend
of flavors.

Nutritional Analysis per Biscuit
Calories: 40, Total Fat: 5.2 g., Saturated Fat: 3.1 g.
Cholesterol: 24 mg., Carbohydrate: 10.3 g., Dietary Fiber: .1 g.
Protein: 1.9 g., Sodium: 187 mg.

ORANGE CURRANT SCONES

Your kitchen will be prefumed with fresh and mouth-watering scents when you make these tasty scones from a recipe by my brother Greg and his wife Kris, who live on the Oregon Coast.

2	cups all-purpose flour
1-1/2	T. baking powder
1/3	cup sugar
1/2	tsp. salt
	Grated peel of 1 orange
6	T. butter
4	T. shortening
1/2	cup buttermilk
1/3	cup currants

Preheat oven to 425° F. Combine flour, baking powder, sugar, salt and orange peel. Cut in butter and shortening. Add buttermilk, stirring gently until just mixed. Fold in currants. Roll out dough 1/2-inch thick. Cut scones into triangles or use biscuit cutter. Brush with a little buttermilk and bake 15 minutes on a greased baking sheet. Makes 12 scones.

Nutritional Analysis per Scone
Calories: 202, Total Fat: 10.3 g., Saturated Fat: 4.7 g.
Cholesterol: 16 mg., Carbohydrate: 25.6 g., Dietary Fiber: .3 g.
Protein: 2.7 g., Sodium: 294 mg.

CHILI-CHEESE SCONES

*My parents, Warner and Edythe Foster, do not drink tea,
and my mother only drinks one cup of coffee in the morning.
This scone recipe of hers is especially good as a companion to her
wonderful soups, stews and chowders.*

1-1/2	cups all-purpose flour
1/4	cup yellow cornmeal
1	tsp. baking powder
1/2	tsp. crushed dried hot chiles
1/4	tsp. ground cumin
1/4	cup butter, cut in pieces
1/4	lb. cheddar cheese
1	egg
1/4	cup milk

Mix all dry ingredients together in a large bowl until well combined. Add butter and mix with your fingers or with a pastry cutter until coarse crumbs form.

Shred the cheese and stir it into the flour mixture. Beat egg and milk to blend, set aside 2 tablespoons of this mixture. Add the remaining egg/milk mixture to the flour mixture and stir until just moistened. Place dough on floured surface and knead 5-6 times, then pat into a 3/4" thick round approximately 6" in diameter. With a knife, cut each round not quite through to form 6 wedges. Brush with reserved egg mixture. Bake at 400° F. until golden brown, about 16 minutes. Scones are best served warm.

*Nutritional Analysis per Serving
Calories: 221, Total Fat: 9.2 g., Saturated Fat: 5.2 g.
Cholesterol: 57 mg., Carbohydrate: 29.1 g., Dietary Fiber: .4 g.
Protein: 5.2 g., Sodium: 154 mg.*

SUTTON AFTERNOON TEA SCONES

Sutton Place Hotel • Vancouver, B.C.

This recipe was brought to the Sutton Place Hotel from London, like so many other good things.

4	cups all purpose flour
1	T. baking powder
1/2	cup butter
1	cup sugar
3	eggs
7	oz. milk (7/8 cup)

Preheat oven to 400° F. In a large bowl sift the flour and baking powder together. With a pastry blender cut the butter into the mixture until it resembles coarse meal. Add the eggs and milk and mix with a fork until a soft pliable dough forms.

On a lightly floured surface roll out the dough to a 1/2" thickness. Cut out the shape with a cookie cutter. Brush the tops with an egg wash.

Heat an ungreased baking sheet in the oven until warm, place the scones on the sheet and bake near the top of the oven until they are a light golden brown about 10 to 15 minutes.

Remove the scones from the baking sheet and serve with Devonshire cream and your favorite preserves.

Makes 12 scones.

Nutritional Analysis per Serving
Calories: 390, Total Fat: 14 g., Saturated Fat: 8.1 g.
Cholesterol: 93 mg., Carbohydrate: 55.5 g., Dietary Fiber: 0 g.
Protein: 10.6 g., Sodium: 254 mg.

SAN JUAN ISLAND CHEESE ROLLS

"Many's the long night I've dreamed of cheese - toasted, mostly."
Robert Louis Stevenson
Treasure Island

    1   cup milk
    2   T. butter
    1/8 tsp. salt
    1/8 tsp. pepper
    1   cup all-purpose flour
    4   eggs
    3/4 cup grated sharp cheddar

Preheat oven to 375° F. Combine milk, butter, salt and pepper in a pan and bring to a boil over medium heat, stirring constantly. Remove from heat, add flour and stir until mixture forms a ball. Beat in eggs until the dough is smooth, then add 1/2 cup grated cheese. Spoon equal portions into 4 well-greased 6 oz. custard cups. Cover tops with remaining cheese. Bake 45 minutes.

Makes 4 rolls.

Nutritional Analysis per Serving
Calories: 362, Total Fat: 20.1 g., Saturated Fat: 10.9 g.
Cholesterol: 258 mg., Carbohydrate: 27.6 g., Dietary Fiber: 0.0 g.
Protein: 16.8 g., Sodium: 350 mg.

ECCLES CAKES

The ovens of the village of Eccles in Lancashire, England gave birth to these traditional teatime treats.

1-3/4	cups all purpose flour
2-1/4	tsp. baking powder
1	T. sugar
1/4	tsp. salt
1/4	cup butter
2	eggs, beaten
1/3	cup half and half
2	T. currants
1	tsp. butter
2	T. sugar
	Ground cinnamon

Mix together the flour, baking powder, 1 T. sugar, and salt. With a pastry blender, cut the 1/4 cup butter until the mixture resembles coarse meal. Set aside 2 tsp. of the beaten egg and mix remaining egg with the cream. Make a well in the center of the flour mixture, add egg-cream mixture and stir until just blended. Turn dough out on a lightly floured board and knead lightly (about 15 times) until dough is no longer sticky.

Roll out dough to 3/4 " thickness and using a biscuit cutter, cut 2-1/2" rounds and place them about 2" apart of greased baking sheet. Reroll scraps.

Poke a hole into the center of each round, fill with 1 tsp. currants and a pea-size dollop of butter. Pinch opposite edges of circle together in the center, enclosing currants in dough (dough will pull apart slightly while baking to form an 'X' on top.)

Brush tops of Eccles cake with reserved egg, and sprinkle with cinnamon-sugar. Bake at 450° F. for 12 minutes, or until golden. Makes 6 Eccles Cakes, which are best served freshly baked or warm.

Nutritional Analysis per Serving
Calories: 281, Total Fat: 11.8 g., Saturated Fat: 6.6 g.
Cholesterol: 98 mg., Carbohydrate: 37.6 g., Dietary Fiber: .3 g.
Protein: 6.5 g., Sodium: 336 mg.

YES! YOU CAN MAKE YOUR OWN CRUMPETS!

Teach us delight in simple things.
Rudyard Kipling

1/2	oz. dry yeast
1	tsp. sugar
3-1/2	cups warm water
4	cups all-purpose flour
2	T. baking powder
1-1/2	tsp. salt

Dissolve yeast and sugar in warm water. Add the flour, baking powder and salt. Whisk together until well blended.

Heat griddle to 450° F. Grease inside of crumpet rings (or clean tuna cans from which you have cut both the top and the bottom). Place rings on heated griddle and pour in 3/4 cup batter.

Cook until bubbles form and the top dries. Remove ring and turn the crumpet to brown lightly.

Makes 2 dozen crumpets which can later be toasted prior to serving.

Nutritional Analysis per Serving
Calories: 79, Total Fat: .2 g., Saturated Fat: 0 g.
Cholesterol: 0 mg., Carbohydrate: 16.6 g., Dietary Fiber: .2 g.
Protein: 2.4 g., Sodium: 226 mg.

IRISH SODA BREAD

*My great-grandfather, John Foster, immigrated from Ireland to settle in
Canada. He played a fiddle, smoked a pipe,
and dearly loved this Soda Bread.*

3	cups flour
1/2	cup sugar
1	T. caraway seed
1	T. baking powder
1	tsp. salt
1	tsp. baking soda
3/4	lb. raisins
1-3/4	cup buttermilk
2	eggs
1	T. melted butter or margarine

Preheat oven to 350° F. Combine the flour, sugar, cara-
way seed, baking powder, salt, baking soda and raisins in
bowl and mix well. Beat buttermilk and eggs together in
a separate bowl for about 30 seconds. Add the butter or
margarine, beating for 10 seconds. Stir this into the flour
mixture.

Spoon the dough into a greased and floured loaf pan or
cast iron skillet. Bake for about 50 minutes. Yields
about 20 slices per loaf.

Nutritional Analysis per Serving
Calories: 161, Total Fat: 1.6 g., Saturated Fat: .7 g.
Cholesterol: 24 mg., Carbohydrate: 34.2 g., Dietary Fiber: .8 g.
Protein: 3.9 g., Sodium: 261 mg.

PEACH BREAD

1/2	cup butter, softened
1	cup sugar
3	eggs
2-3/4	cups flour
1-1/2	tsp. baking powder
1/2	tsp. baking soda
1	tsp. salt
1-1/2	tsp. ground cinnamon
1/4	tsp. nutmeg
2	cups coarsely chopped fresh peaches
3	T. frozen orange juice concentrate, thawed
1	tsp. vanilla

Preheat oven to 350° F. Grease and flour two loaf pans. Cream butter and sugar, beating well. Add eggs one at a time, beating well after each is added.

Combine all dry ingredients and add alternately to creamed mixture with peaches, beginning and ending with dry ingredients. Stir in orange juice and vanilla.

Pour into prepared pans and bake 50 - 60 minutes until tester comes out clean. Cool 10 minutes before turning out of pans. Cool completely before slicing.

Makes 24 servings.

Nutritional Analysis per Serving
Calories: 138, Total Fat: 4.6 g., Saturated Fat: 2.6 g.
Cholesterol: 37 mg., Carbohydrate: 22 g., Dietary Fiber: .4 g.
Protein: 2.5 g., Sodium: 185 mg.

COCONUT BREAD

2-3/4	cup all-purpose flour
1-1/2	cup milk
1	cup sugar
1	egg, lightly beaten
1	T. + 1 tsp. baking powder
2	T. peanut oil
1	tsp. salt
1	tsp. coconut extract
1-1/4	cup shredded coconut, toasted and cooled

Preheat oven to 350° F. Lightly coat a loaf pan with vegetable spray. Sift flour, baking powder and salt into a medium bowl. Add toasted coconut and blend well.

Combine milk, egg, oil and extract in another bowl and mix well. Add to dry ingredients all at once, stirring briefly just until blended; do not overmix.

Turn into pan and bake approximately 1 hour or until tester comes out clean when inserted in center.

20 servings

Nutritional Analysis per Serving
Calories: 158, Total Fat: 4.4 g., Saturated Fat: 2.5 g.
Cholesterol: 13 mg., Carbohydrate: 27 g., Dietary Fiber: .3 g.
Protein: 2.9 g., Sodium: 207 mg.

PUMPKIN BREAD

2	tsp. ground cinnamon
2	tsp. baking powder
1	tsp. nutmeg
1	tsp. baking soda
1	tsp. salt
1/2	tsp. ground cloves
1/4	tsp. ground ginger
	dash allspice
6	cups unbleached white flour
1	cup vegetable oil
1/2	cup plain yogurt
4	eggs
3	cups sugar
2-1/2	cups unsweetened pumpkin puree
1	cup chopped walnuts or pecans

Preheat oven to 350° F. In a large bowl, sift together cinnamon, baking powder, nutmeg, baking soda, salt, cloves, ginger, allspice, and flour. Set aside.

In a separate bowl, mix together the oil, eggs, yogurt, sugar, and pumpkin. Mix until smooth.

Combine the two mixtures and beat until smooth, then fold in the chopped nuts. Pour the batter into three loaf pans. Bake for 45 minutes to 1 hour. Loaves are done when they have a hollow sound when tapped. Makes three loaves that freeze well. Yields 20 slices per loaf.

Nutritional Analysis per Slice
Calories: 134, Total Fat: 5.5 g., Saturated Fat: .7 g.
Cholesterol: 14 mg., Carbohydrate: 20 g., Dietary Fiber: 1.9 g.
Protein: 2.8 g., Sodium: 75 mg.

REBECCA'S BUTTER TART MUFFINS

Secret Garden • Vancouver, B.C.

"I do like a little bit of butter to my bread!"
A. A. Milne

1-1/2 cups raisins
3/4 cup sugar
1/2 cup butter cut into chunks
2 eggs beaten
1/2 cup milk
1 tsp. vanilla
1/2 cup all purpose flour
2 tsp. baking powder
1 tsp. baking soda
pinch salt
1/2 cup chopped walnuts or pecans
1/4 cup corn or maple syrup

Place raisins, sugar, butter, eggs, milk and vanilla in large heavy-bottomed saucpan. Place over medium heat and cook, stirring frequently, until mixture is hot, slightly thickened, and just beginning to bubble, about 4 to 5 minutes. Cool slightly uncovered in the refrigerator.

Preheat oven to 375° F. Grease 12 muffin cups or spray coat with cooking spray. Combine flour, baking powder, soda and salt in large mixing bowl, make a well in center and pour in warm raisin mixture, stirring until just combined. Stir in nuts until evenly mixed.

Spoon batter into muffin cups. Bake until golden and cake tester comes out clean, about 15 to 17 minutes. Remove from oven and immediately pour about one teaspoon syrup over each muffin. Cool muffins in cups about 10 minutes then remove to a rack. Best served warm. Freeze well too!

Serve with Secret Garden English Breakfast Tea

Nutritional Analysis per Serving
Calories: 259, Total Fat: 11.8 g., Saturated Fat: 5.4 g.
Cholesterol: 57 mg., Carbohydrate: 37.5 g., Dietary Fiber: 1.0 g.
Protein: 3.8 g., Sodium: 291 mg.

FRESH STRAWBERRY MUFFINS

*"Doubtless God could have made a better berry [strawberry],
but doubtless God never did."*
William Butler
Walton, The Compleat Angler

1/2	cup butter, softened
1	cup sugar
2	eggs
2	cups flour
2	tsp. baking powder
1/4	tsp. salt
2/3	cup milk
1	tsp. grated lemon rind
1	cup fresh strawberries, chopped
1	T. cinnamon sugar

Preheat oven to 375° F. Grease or line muffin pan with paper liners. Cream butter in large bowl, gradually adding sugar and eggs, creaming until light and fluffy.

Sift together flour, baking powder and salt. Add to creamed mixture alternately with milk, beginning and ending with the dry ingredients. Stir in lemon rind and gently fold in berries.

Spoon batter into muffin pans, filling each 2/3 full. Sprinkle cinnamon sugar lightly over top of batter. Bake 15 to 18 minutes. Makes 12 muffins.

Nutritional Analysis per Serving
Calories: 236, Total Fat: 9.1 g., Saturated Fat: 5.3 g.
Cholesterol: 58 mg., Carbohydrate: 35.5 g., Dietary Fiber: .4 g.
Protein: 3.8 g., Sodium: 200 mg.

GRANDMA & GRANDPA'S BLUEBERRY MUFFINS

The Little Tea Room • Puyallup, Washington

Childhood visits to the Montana woods cottage of their grandparents inspired sisters, Darlene and Angela, to recreate these muffins.

4	eggs
1	cup margarine
1	cup sugar
2	tsp. vanilla
1	pint sour cream
2-1/2	cups flour
1/2	tsp. soda
1	tsp. baking powder
1	pint fresh or frozen blueberries

Beat eggs until stiff, set aside. Mix margarine and sugar thoroughly. Add vanilla and sour cream, mix thoroughly. Add eggs.

Mix flour, soda and baking powder them add to mixture. Fold in blueberries. Granulated sugar can be added to tops before baking at 400° F. for 15-20 minutes. Makes 2 dozen regular muffins.

Nutritional Analysis per Muffin
Calories: 176, Total Fat: 12.6 g., Saturated Fat: 4.1 g.
Cholesterol: 44 mg., Carbohydrate: 12.7 g., Dietary Fiber: .3 g.
Protein: 3.2 g., Sodium: 152 mg.

BEA BOTHELL'S EXCELLENT PIE CRUST

(because Moody Pie Crust sounds uncooperative)

When we bought the property on Camano Island where Ken built our home, our first happy coincidence was to discover that our new next-door neighbor, Irene Moody, was from Ken's hometown, Liverpool, England! Irene's fresh blackberry pies every summer are the stuff of legends, and her pie crust is the very best we've ever had.

This pie crust recipe is from Irene's yankee husband, Pat, retired Assistant Fire Chief of Seattle, (so don't overcook it). Pat is the great-great-great-great grandson of the founder of Bothell, Washington, and this recipe originated with his great-great grandmother, so we named it after her.

2	cups flour
1/2	tsp. salt
1/4	tsp. baking powder
1	cup shortening (she uses Crisco)
	a small glass of ice water

Mix the salt and baking powder together and add to the 2 cups of flour you've placed in a bowl. Cut in 1 cup of shortening and then dive in with your hands to mix lightly until the texture is crumbly. Add ice water until the dough is the consistency to roll. Do all this quickly, because the least this dough is handled the lighter and flakier it will be. Roll on floured surface.

Makes a double crust for a 9" fruit pie.

COOKIES & BARS

BUTTER ROUNDS FILLED COOKIES

Our friend, Judy Judson Carroll, is such a good cook, that when she gets excited about a recipe, you know you better listen. Recipes flow through Judy from a myriad of sources, including her Cordon Bleu-trained daughter with whom she is co-authoring a cookbook. This one, however, originated with the mother of the mechanic who keeps her car running:

Cookie:
>   1   cup butter or margarine
>   2   cups sifted flour
>   1/3   cup heavy cream

Mix well and chill thoroughly. Roll thinly on a board dusted with a mixture of 1/2 flour and 1/2 sugar, using small amount of dough at a time. Cut into 2" circle and prick twice with a fork. Bake at 375° F. on ungreased sheet 7 to 9 minutes. Let cool on rack completely. In the meantime, make the filling:

Filling:
>   1/4   cup butter
>   3/4   cup sifted powdered sugar
>   1   egg yolk
>   1   tsp. vanilla

Do not chill the filling recipe. It's easier to spread on the cookie round when at room temperature. Sandwich a dollop of filling between two cookies rounds. Makes 36.

Nutritional Analysis per Cookie
Calories: 100, Total Fat: 7.3 g., Saturated Fat: 4.5 g.
Cholesterol: 26 mg., Carbohydrate: 7.9 g., Dietary Fiber: 0 g.
Protein: .9 g., Sodium: 65 mg.

Note: some cooks prefer not to use uncooked fresh egg products in their recipes due to risk of salmonella. Several pastuerized egg substitutes are now available to use in recipes such as this one.

GINGER SHORTBREAD

Crystallized ginger chunks make the difference in this rich shortbread.

        1-1/4   cup all-purpose flour
         1/3   cup sugar
         1/2   cup unsalted butter, cut in pieces
           3   T. crystallized ginger, chopped fine
         1/2   tsp. ground ginger

Preheat oven to 325° F. In a bowl, combine the flour, both the crystallized and ground ginger, 1/4 cup of the sugar , and the butter. Crumble with your fingers and press into a firm lump with your hands.

Spread this crumbly dough in a 8" or 9" springform pan, pressing out evenly and firmly. Prick the surface with a fork. Bake about 40 minutes. Cut while warm into 8 to 12 wedges.

Sprinkle with remaining sugar, let cool, then remove the pan sides. Store in airtight container.

Nutritional Analysis per Serving
Calories: 150, Total Fat: 8.3 g., Saturated Fat: 5.1 g.
Cholesterol: 24 mg., Carbohydrate: 15.5 g., Dietary Fiber: 0 g.
Protein: 1.4 g., Sodium: 1 mg.

Wild Blackberry Lemon Bars

Each summer on Camano Island the deer and I await the glorious ripening of overgrown blackberries on our neighbor's vacant property. The deer, followed by Ken with his cereal bowl, usually get there first, but there's always enough to go around.

1	cup butter, softened
3/4	cup sifted powdered sugar
2	cups all-purpose flour
4	eggs
1-1/2	cup granulated sugar
1/3	cup juice of fresh lemons
2	T. finely shredded orange peel
1/4	cup all-purpose flour
1	tsp. baking powder
1-1/2	cups fresh wild blackberries
	Powdered sugar

For Crust

Cream butter for 45 seconds to soften and add 3/4 cup powdered sugar, combining well. Add 2 cups flour, mix until combined. Press into bottom of greased 13x9x2 inch baking pan. Bake at 350° F. for 20 minutes.

For Filling

In a large mixing bowl combine granulated sugar, eggs, lemon juice, orange peel, 1/4 cup flour, and baking powder. Beat for 3 minutes until combined.

Sprinkle well-washed and drained berries over cooked crust. Pour filling over berries. Bake 350° F. for 30-35 minutes or until filling is set and lightly browned.

Cool well and cut into bars or triangles. Just before serving, sprinkle with powdered sugar for garnish. Store covered in refrigerator. Makes about 24 bars.

Nutritional Analysis per Serving
Calories: 180, Total Fat: 7.7 g., Saturated Fat: 4.7 g.
Cholesterol: 20 mg., Carbohydrate: 27.4 g., Dietary Fiber: .5 g.
Protein: 1.4 g., Sodium: 78 mg.

JAM DROP COOKIES

Every year I get at least one set of small jars of gourmet jams in interesting flavors as a gift from friends who know better than to give me traditional fruitcake. This recipe provides an excellent way to share that largesse with other friends.

2	sticks unsalted butter
1/2	cup sugar
2	egg yolks
1	T. lemon juice
2-1/4	cups all-purpose flour
1-1/2	tsp. baking powder
1/4	tsp. cinnamon
1/4	tsp. cardamom
1/4	tsp. salt
	Assorted interesting jams and jellies you already have in your refrigerator.

Preheat oven to 350° F. Cream the butter and sugar. Add egg yolks and lemon juice and beat until smooth. Add all the remaining ingredients and form into a ball.

Form into small balls, approximately 1 tablespoon each, and place in miniature muffin paper cups (available at kitchen and gourmet stores). Make a thumbprint on each, and place a dollop of jam or jelly in each. Variety is the spice of life! Bake for 30 minutes or until golden.

Makes 3 dozen cookies.

Nutritional Analysis per Cookie
Calories: 85, Total Fat: 5.2 g., Saturated Fat: 3.2 g.
Cholesterol: 14 mg., Carbohydrate: 9 g., Dietary Fiber: 0 g.
Protein: .9 g., Sodium: 82 mg.

HONEY MADELEINES

Heavenly Tea and Gifts • Vancouver, Washington

>   1/4   cup butter, melted
>   2   eggs
>   1/4   cup sugar
>   1   T. honey
>   1/2   cup all-purpose flour
>   1/2   tsp. baking powder
> (We also add a touch of fresh lemon rind for flavor)

Beat eggs with sugar until pale and thick, then stir in melted butter and honey. Sift flour and baking powder onto egg mixture, then fold in.

Spoon mixture into prepared molds and bake 10 minutes at 350° F. until light golden brown. Leave in molds 2 minutes then turn out and transfer to a wire rack to cool.

To finish, dust lightly with powered sugar. Makes about 2 dozen small Madeleines or 1 dozen large.

Can also be made in tartlet pans.

 TEA NOTE
The owner of Heavenly Tea & Gifts, Cathy Loendorf, recommends either an afternoon black tea or a mango flavored tea blend to accompany these.

Nutritional Analysis per Serving
Calories: 43, Total Fat: 2.3 g., Saturated Fat: 1.3 g.
Cholesterol: 23 mg., Carbohydrate: 4.9 g., Dietary Fiber: 0.0 g.
Protein: .8 g., Sodium: 32 mg.

CHOCOLATE CHIP MERINGUE BARS

Our dear friend Terry Dean, who helped Ken build our house, loves chocolate and Martha Stewart, in that order. I think he should send these bars to her, he just might win her over with his recipe.

1/2	cup butter
1/2	cup sugar
1/2	cup brown sugar
2	egg yolks
1	T. water
1	tsp. vanilla
2	cups flour
1/4	tsp. salt
1/4	tsp. baking soda
1	tsp. baking powder
1	12 oz. package chocolate chips
	or one 12 oz. bar semi-sweet chocolate

Topping:

2	egg whites
1	cup brown sugar

Preheat oven to 350° F. Lightly grease 15" jellyroll pan.

In large bowl, cream together butter and sugars; add egg yolks, water and vanilla. Mix well. Mix together flour, salt, baking soda, and baking powder. Add to butter mixture. Pat dough into pan and sprinkle evenly with chocolate chips.

Make topping: in small bowl of mixer, beat egg whites until stiff. Gradually beat in brown sugar. Spread mixture over top of chocolate chips. Bake 20 to 25 minutes.

Cool, then cut into 24 bars.

Nutritional Analysis per Serving
Calories: 196, Total Fat: 8.5 g., Saturated Fat: 5.0 g.
Cholesterol: 28 mg., Carbohydrate: 30 g., Dietary Fiber: .8 g.
Protein: 2.2 g., Sodium: 100 mg.

TINY PECAN PIES

*Jacque Chase is one of those marvelously balanced people.
A successful business woman, mother, decorator, and gardener;
she found the love of her life in our neighbor Bob Chase a year ago and
retired happily every after to her lovely Camano Island view home.
She's even a gourmet cook.....*

24 Pastry Shells:
1/2 cup butter or margarine
  3 oz. soft cream cheese
  1 cup flour

Mix softened cream cheese and butter in a small bowl
until smooth. Add flour, mixing well. Chill dough 1
hour. Shape dough into 24 - 1 inch balls. Place each ball
in an ungreased 1 3/4" muffin tin and shape into a shell.

Filling:
3/4 cup brown sugar firmly packed
      pinch salt
  1 T. butter
  1 tsp. vanilla
  1 egg
2/3 cup chopped pecans

Combine brown sugar, butter, egg, salt and vanilla in a
mixing bowl. Beat at medium speed with an electric
mixer until smooth. Layer 1/2 teaspoon of chopped
pecans in bottom of each pastry shell. Add 1 teaspoon of
filling and 1/2 teaspoon of pecans. Bake in 325° F. oven
for 25 minutes.

Yield: 24 Tiny Pies.

*Nutritional Analysis per Serving
Calories: 109, Total Fat: 7.8 g., Saturated Fat: 3.7 g.
Cholesterol: 24 mg., Carbohydrate: 9.1 g., Dietary Fiber: .2 g.
Protein: 1.3 g., Sodium: 69 mg.*

RUSSIAN TEA CAKES

Lisa's Tea Treasures • Bellevue, Washington

Lisa's Tea Treasures manager Kemberli Paffendorf shares this recipe from her beloved grandmother.

1	lb. butter
8	oz. sugar
1	oz. vanilla
1-1/2	lb. flour
1/4	oz. salt
6	oz. chopped pecans

Cream butter and sugar in mixer until light and fluffy. Add vanilla and mix in.

In a separate bowl mix together flour, salt and nuts. Blend in dry ingredients with butter/sugar mixture only until incorporated.

Drop tablespoons of dough evenly spaced on a sheetpan.

Bake at 325° F. for 10 minutes only. Remove from oven, cool totally. Store in a sealed container.

Just before serving roll in powdered sugar. Makes 48.

TEA NOTE
Kemberli recommends serving these treats with an exotic Russian Caravan tea.

Nutritional Analysis per Serving
Calories: 164, Total Fat: 10.2 g., Saturated Fat: 5.0 g.
Cholesterol: 21 mg., Carbohydrate: 16.5 g., Dietary Fiber: .3 g.
Protein: 1.8 g., Sodium: 136 mg.

BRENDA'S LEMON SQUARES

The Country Register Cafe and Tea Room • Kennewick, Washington

Crust
  2   cups flour
1/2 cup powdered sugar
  1   cup butter (softened)

Blend together and press into a small sheet pan. Bake 10 minutes at 350° F.

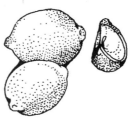

Filling
  8   eggs
  2   tsp. grated lemon rind
  3   cups sugar
3/4 cup lemon juice
  1   tsp. baking powder
1/2 cup sifted flour

Beat eggs together with lemon rind, sugar and lemon juice. Stir baking powder and flour into above mixture. Spread over crust and bake 20 to 30 minutes at 350° F. Sprinkle powdered sugar on top after bars have cooled. 36 servings

TEA NOTE
Try these tasty lemon squares with Earl Grey tea.

Nutritional Analysis per Square
Calories: 165, Total Fat: 6.2 g., Saturated Fat: 3.5 g.
Cholesterol: 61 mg., Carbohydrate: 25.6 g., Dietary Fiber: 0 g.
Protein: 2.4 g., Sodium: 76 mg.

BUTTERSCOTCH PECAN DIAMONDS

Village Tea Room • Edmonds, Washington

The favorite recipe of the Village Tea Room in Edmonds originated with Karen Giordano, noted tea expert and author who lives on Whidbey Island. This recipe appears in her book "Easy Tea Treats for Busy Tea Lovers!"

1	pkg yellow cake mix
3/4	cup shortening
2	egg yolks
1	T. milk
2	egg whites
2	T. water
1-1/4	cup ground pecans or walnuts

Preheat oven to 375° F. Combine dry cake mix, shortening, egg yolks and milk.

Spray large cookie sheet with oilspray, and line cookie sheet with waxed paper, let 2" project over sides, spray waxed paper.

Pat dough into cookie sheet (it will be thin). Beat egg whites and water slightly. Brush top of dough with egg white mixture. Press nuts evenly over the top. Bake about 15 minutes or until golden brown.

Cool 10 minutes. Have cutting board or pastry sheet ready.

Turn pan over onto board or sheet. Peel off waxed paper. Cut immediately in diagonal lines to form diamonds.

Makes about 24. Store in airtight container.

Nutritional Analysis per serving:
Calories: 194, Total Fat: 13.2 g., Saturated Fat: 2.4 g.
Cholesterol: 18 mg., Carbohydrate: 17.9 g., Dietary Fiber: .4 g.
Protein: 1.9 g., Sodium: 147 mg.

DANISH APPLE BARS

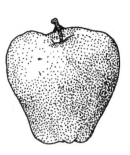

2-1/2	cup flour
1	cup margarine
1/2	tsp. salt
1	egg
2/3	cup milk
1	cup Rice Krispies
6	pared, sliced apples
3/4	cup sugar
1	tsp. cinnamon

Glaze:

1/2	cup powdered sugar,
1	tsp. vanilla
	milk to moisten to drizzle consistency.

Mix until crumbly: 2-1/2 cups flour, 1 cup margarine, and 1/2 tsp. salt. Beat 1 egg yolk (save the white for later in the recipe) with 2/3 cup milk. Add to the flour mixture and knead just til mixed in. Cut the dough in half and roll one half into a rectangle and put on a cookie sheet.

Sprinkle 1 cup of crushed Rice Krsipies over this crust. On top of that arrange 6 pared, and sliced apples. Over the top of that, sprinkle a mixture of 3/4 cup sugar and 1 tsp. cinnamon.

Roll out the other half of the dough and lay over the top of the filling. Trim and pinch edges to seal as you would a pie. Brush with egg white and sprinkle with sugar. Bake at 350° F. for about 30 minutes.

As soon as it comes out of the oven, drizzle the entire top with a mixture of 1 cup powdered sugar, 1 tsp. vanilla, and just enough milk to make runny. Cut into 18 bars.

Nutritional Analysis per Serving
Calories: 287, Total Fat: 11.4 g., Saturated Fat: 2.2 g.
Cholesterol: 13 mg., Carbohydrate: 43.4 g., Dietary Fiber: 1.9 g.
Protein: 3.7 g., Sodium: 229 mg.

CAKES & TARTS

SUMMER FRUIT CAKE

*Every Christmas I used to wear a button that read "Get Even.
Give Fruitcake." Even if you think you hate fruitcake,
this fresh fruit version will convert you.*

Cake		Glaze
2	cup whole wheat flour	2/3 cup sugar
1-1/2	cups sugar	1/3 cup buttermilk
1	tsp. baking soda	1/3 cup butter
1	tsp. cinnamon	2 T. light corn syrup
1/2	tsp. salt	
1/4	tsp. baking soda	
3	eggs	
1/2	tsp. vanilla	
3/4	cup buttermilk	
1/2	cup vegetable oil	
2	tsp. vanilla	
2-1/2	cups fresh apricots, peaches and/or plums chopped and drained	
1	cup chopped pecans	
1	cup flaked coconut	
1	cup raisins	

For the cake: Preheat oven to 350° F. Grease and flour a
9" x 13" baking dish, shaking out excess flour. Combine
flour, sugar, baking soda, cinnamon and salt in medium
bowl. Beat eggs, buttermilk, oil and vanilla in a large
bowl. Add flour mixture to eggs and mix until smooth.
Stir in remaining ingredients. Pour into baking dish and
bake about 40 to 45 min. until tester inserted in center
comes out clean. While cake is baking, prepare glaze.

For the glaze: Combine all ingredients except the vanilla
in a saucepan and bring to a boil over medium heat. Stir
5 minutes. Remove from heat. Add vanilla and blend
thoroughly. Poke entire surface of cake with toothpick.
Pour glaze slowly and evenly over top. Let cool completely. Makes 15 Servings

*Nutritional Analysis per Serving
Calories: 410, Total Fat: 19.4 g., Saturated Fat: 5.6 g.
Cholesterol: 54 mg., Carbohydrate: 57.9 g., Dietary Fiber: 3.8 g.
Protein: 5.5 g., Sodium: 267 mg.*

BISHOP'S CAKE

There is an old Irish country superstition of "nipping the cake."
This was the custom of breaking off a small piece of cake when fresh
from the oven, to avert bad luck.

3	eggs, well beaten
1	cup sugar
1-1/2	cups flour
1/4	tsp. salt
6	oz. chocolate chips
2	cups coarsely chopped walnuts
1	cup pitted dates, cut up
1	cup candied cherries or maraschino cherries, halved

Preheat oven to 325° F. Grease loaf pan and line it with waxed paper; grease waxed paper. Cream together eggs and sugar, beating until thick.

Sift together flour, baking powder, and salt over the bowl of fruit, nuts and chocolate chips. Mix well. Combine with egg/sugar mixture and pour into prepared pan.

Bake for approximately 1-1/4 to 1-1/2 hours or until tester is clean. Cool on wire rack. Cake will have crusty top. Remove from pan when completely cool. Serves 12.

Nutritional Analysis per Serving
Calories: 399, Total Fat: 17.5 g., Saturated Fat: 3.7 g.
Cholesterol: 53 mg., Carbohydrate: 57.3 g., Dietary Fiber: 3.2 g.
Protein: 9.2 g., Sodium: 73 mg.

JUDITH'S SWEDISH CREAM CAKE

Judith's Tearooms and Rose Cafe • Poulsbo, Washington

Judith Goodrich ate a piece of cake in Ballard once that set her upon a quest to recreate the recipe. After eight different cakes, she created, in her own words, "cake so delicious that tears will come to your eyes when you take your first bite." This recipe is from Judith's cookbook "Favorite Recipes from Judith's."

	Yellow cake (homemade, or boxed without pudding in the mix)
2	T. sour cream or cream cheese
1/2	cup cream sherry
	dried apricots
	freshly whipped cream

Follow recipe for yellow cake and add two tablespoons of sour cream or cream cheese to the cake batter while it is mixing. Pour into prepared tube pan or angel food cake pan. Place on center rack in 350 F. oven. The cake will take anywhere from 35 to 70 minutes depending on how full your pan is. Remove and let cool for about 15 minutes.

Pour 1/2 cup cream sherry over the cake. Let it soak in and cool in the pan. Remove from the pan when completely cool and slice horizontally. Fill with freshly whipped cream and dried apricots that have been plumped with cream sherry for at least four hours.

Makes 18 servings.

Nutritional Analysis per Serving
Calories: 213, Total Fat: 10.5 g., Saturated Fat: 3.7 g.
Cholesterol: 35 mg., Carbohydrate: 26.1 g., Dietary Fiber: .4 g.
Protein: 2.6 g., Sodium: 177 mg.

Butternut and Vanilla Cake

Tudor Rose Tea Room • Salem, Oregon

1/2 cup shortening
2 sticks margarine
3 cups sugar
3 cups flour
1 cup milk
6 eggs
3 tsp. Butternut Vanilla flavoring.

Heat oven 325° F. Grease 10 in. tube pan and dust with flour. Mix all shortening, margarine. eggs and sugar together. Add a little flour to stop curdling. Add milk and rest of flour.

Bake for 1-1/2 hours. Makes 18 servings.

TEA NOTE
*Mrs. Jones recommends Typhoo P. G. Tips
as the perfect tea to serve with this rich cake.*

*Nutritional Analysis per Serving
Calories: 293, Total Fat: 8.4 g., Saturated Fat: 2.3 g.
Cholesterol: 73 mg., Carbohydrate: 50.1 g., Dietary Fiber: 0 g.
Protein: 4.7 g., Sodium: 33 mg.*

SNOHOMISH
GINGER PEACH CAKE

2 fresh peaches
1/2 cup all-purpose flour
1 cup firmly packed dark brown sugar
1/2 cup shortening
2 eggs
1/2 tsp. baking soda
1/4 cup molasses
2-1/2 cup all-purpose flour, sifted
1 tsp. baking powder
1/2 tsp. allspice
1/2 tsp. cinnamon
1 tsp. ginger
1/2 tsp. salt
3/4 cup milk
Powdered sugar

Preheat oven to 375. Place sliced peaches in bowl and sprinkle in 1 cup flour. Cream the brown sugar and shortening until fluffy, then beat in eggs. Add baking soda to the molasses and stir into sugar mixture.

Sift together the flour, baking powder, allspice, cinnamon, ginger, and salt.

Add to the creamed mixture alternating with milk until well blended.

Add peaches and pour into a greased and floured ring pan. Bake 40 minutes or until tester inserted in center comes out clean. Sprinkle with powdered sugar.

Serve with whipped cream or sour cream sweetened with a little sugar. Serves 12.

Nutritional Analysis per Serving
Calories: 263, Total Fat: 10.2 g., Saturated Fat: 2.8 g.
Cholesterol: 37 mg., Carbohydrate: 37.9 g., Dietary Fiber: .4 g.
Protein: 4.9 g., Sodium: 193 mg.

Fresh Orange Buttermilk Cake

1 orange	1/4 tsp. baking soda
1-1/2 cup sugar	1-1/2 tsp. baking powder
1/2 cup butter	1/4 tsp. salt
2 eggs	1 cup buttermilk
2 cups sifted cake flour	

Preheat oven to 350 . Grate the peel, cut orange in half, extract the juice. Add 1/2 cup sugar to the juice and peel. Stir to dissolve. Set aside.

Cream butter until light and fluffy, then add 1 cup sugar and continue to beat until light and creamy. Stir together the cake flour, baking soda, baking powder and the salt. Add these dry ingredients to the creamed mixture alternately with buttermilk, beginning and ending with the flour. Beat only to blend thoroughly. Pour into lightly greaed and floured 9" square pan. Bake 30-35 min. Cool on rack 15 min. Poke holes in top of cake with handle of wooden spoon or skewer and spoon the orange juice mix over top. Slice laterally and fill with the following:

ORANGE FILLING:

1/2 cup sugar	3 T. lemon juice
4 T. cake flour	2 T. water
dash salt	1 beaten egg
1/3 cup orange juice	2 T. butter
1-1/2 tsp. grated orange rind	

Combine sugar, flour, and salt in top of double boiler, add fruit juices, water, egg. Place over rapidly boiling water and cook 10 minutes, stirring occasionally. Remove from double boiler, add butter and orange rind. Cool and spread between the split layers of the Orange Buttermilk Cake. Reassemble cake. Serves 9.

Nutritional Analysis per Serving
Calories: 341, Total Fat: 11.7 g., Saturated Fat: 6.8 g.
Cholesterol: 75 mg., Carbohydrate: 55.5 g., Dietary Fiber: .8 g.
Protein: 4.5 g., Sodium: 301 mg.

APPLE-MAPLE CAKE

"Autumn evening, and the morn
When the golden mists are born."
Percy Bysshe Shelley

1-1/2	cups all-purpose flour
1	tsp. baking powder
1/2	tsp. baking soda
1/4	tsp. salt
1	beaten egg
1-1/2	cups peeled, cored, and chopped baking apple
1/2	cup sugar
1/2	cup pure maple syrup
1/2	cup raisins
1/3	cup applesauce
1/3	cup cooking oil
1-1/2	tsp. grated orange peel
	Pure maple syrup
	Whipping cream
	Sour cream

Spray 8-inch square baking pan with nonstick coating. In a bowl combine the flour, baking powder, baking soda, and the salt.

In a large bowl combine the beaten egg and the apples. Stir in sugar, 1/2 cup maple syrup, raisins, applesauce and orange peel. Add the dry ingredients and stir until just combined. Spread better in the prepared pan.

Bake at 350° F. for 40 to 45 minutes or until toothpick comes out clean. Brush the warm cake with additional maple syrup and cool slightly. Serve warm or at room temperature with Maple Cream. Makes 9 servings.

Maple Cream - In a chilled mixing bowl beat 1/2 cup whipping cream on medium speed until stiff peaks form. Stir together 1/2 cup sour cream and 1/4 cup pure maple syrup and fold into whipped cream. Serve immediately.

Nutritional Analysis per Serving
Calories: 394, Total Fat: 16.6 g., Saturated Fat: 5.9 g.
Cholesterol: 47 mg., Carbohydrate: 59.9 g., Dietary Fiber: 1.2 g.
Protein: 3.9 g., Sodium: 192 mg.

MANGO UPSIDE-DOWN CAKE

3	ripe mangos, peeled
1/2	cup unsalted butter + 1/3 cup
3/4	cup light brown sugar
1/4	tsp. cardamon
1/2	cup rum + 1 tsp.
1-2/3	cups flour
2	tsp. baking powder
	pinch of salt
2/3	cup sugar
2	eggs
2/3	cup milk

Cut mangos in strips 1" wide, 3" or 4" long. Melt 1/2 cup butter in a skillet over medium heat. Add mangoes and sprinkle brown sugar and cardamon over top. Cook, stirring gently about 5 minutes. Remove mango with slotted spoon and place aside. Continue to cook the sugar mixture until it gets syrupy, about 5 min. Remove from heat and add rum.

Arrange a single layer of the mango in a starburst pattern in an 8" cake pan. Add enough of the syrup to cover mangoes. Set aside.

Heat oven to 350° F. Sift together flour, baking powder, and salt. Set aside.

Cream another 1/3 cup butter with sugar. Beat in remaining 1 tsp. rum and eggs until fluffy. Add flour mixture and milk gradually, beat until smooth.

Spread batter over fruit in cakepan and bake until golden brown 35-40 minutes. Cool on rack for a full 30 minutes before inverting onto cake plate. Serves 12.

Nutritional Analysis per Serving
Calories: 425, Total Fat: 15.4 g., Saturated Fat: 9.0 g.
Cholesterol: 74 mg., Carbohydrate: 61.5 g., Dietary Fiber: .9 g.
Protein: 6.2 g., Sodium: 85 mg.

PINA COLADA CAKE

Serve at your Cinco de Mayo Tea!

3	cups flour
1	tsp. baking soda
1	tsp. salt
1	tsp. cinnamon
2	cups sugar
1-1/2	cups vegetable oil
3	large eggs, lightly beaten
1	8 oz. can crushed pineapple with the liquid
2	cups mashed bananas (about 5 bananas)
3-1/2	oz. flaked coconut
1-1/2	tsp. vanilla

Preheat oven to 350° F. Butter and flour 10" tube pan with removable bottom.

In large bowl sift together first 4 ingredients; add sugar and combine well. In another bowl, combine next 4 ingredients; add to dry ingredients, and stir until just combined. Stir in coconut and vanilla.

Pour into prepared pan and bake 1 hour 10 min. to 1 hour 20 minute or until tester comes out clean. Cool cake on wire rack 15 minutes, then remove from pan.

18 servings.

Nutritional Analysis per Serving
Calories: 400, Total Fat: 21.3 g., Saturated Fat: 4.2 g.
Cholesterol: 35 mg., Carbohydrate: 50.4 g., Dietary Fiber: 1.2 g.
Protein: 3.7 g., Sodium: 214 mg.

APRICOT BRANDY POUND CAKE

My experience convinced me that tea was better than brandy.
Theodore Roosevelt

1	cup butter
3	cups sugar
6	eggs
3	cups flour
1/4	tsp. baking soda
1/2	tsp. salt
1	cup sour cream
1/2	tsp. rum extract
1	tsp. orange extract
1/2	tsp. almond extract
1/2	tsp. lemon extract
1	tsp. vanilla
1/2	cup apricot brandy

Preheat oven to 325° F. Grease and flour a 9" or 10" tube pan. Cream the butter and sugar thoroughly in large bowl. Add eggs one at a time, beating well after each addition.

Sift together flour, soda, and salt three times. Combine sour cream, flavorings and brandy. Add dry ingredients, alternately with sour cream mixture, to butter/sugar/ egg mixture, beginning and ending with dry ingredients.

Pour into prepared pan; bake 60 - 70 minutes.

Cool 15-20 minutes before removing from pan.

Makes 18 servings

Nutritional Analysis per Serving
Calories: 365, Total Fat: 14.7 g., Saturated Fat: 8.5 g.
Cholesterol: 104 mg., Carbohydrate: 50 g., Dietary Fiber: 0.0 g.
Protein: 4.7 g., Sodium: 208 mg.

PEAR WALNUT CAKE

The Pewter Pot • Cashmere, Washington

*The upper Wenatchee Valley, where Cashmere is located,
is one of the world's premier pear-growing regions.
This is one of The Pewter Pot's favorite recipes for pears.*

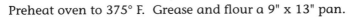

2	cups flour
1	tsp. cinnamon
1	tsp. baking soda
1/2	tsp. nutmeg
1/2	tsp. salt
1/2	cup vegetable oil
1-1/2	cups brown sugar
3	eggs
1/4	cup water
1	tsp. vanilla extract
3	ripe pears, cored and diced with peel on (use Bartlett, d'Anjou, or Bosc pears)

Preheat oven to 375° F. Grease and flour a 9" x 13" pan.

Stir together dry ingredients and set aside. Cream the oil with the sugar and eggs until light and fluffy. Add the water and vanilla and mix well. Stir in dry ingredients.

Add the pears and pour the batter into the prepared pan. Bake for 45 to 55 minutes. Cover with foil if the cake gets too brown during baking. Serve warm with whipped cream or ice cream. Serves 12.

*Nutritional Analysis per Serving
Calories: 269, Total Fat: 10.7 g., Saturated Fat: 1.5 g.
Cholesterol: 53 mg., Carbohydrate: 40.2 g., Dietary Fiber: 1.1 g.
Protein: 3.9 g., Sodium: 217 mg.*

VIENNESE TART

British Pantry • Redmond, Washington

1 lb. butter.
4 oz. powdered sugar.
12 oz. all-purpose flour.
4 oz. corn flour.
1 tsp. vanilla.
  pinch salt.
  raspberry, strawberry
  or apricot jam.
  optional food coloring.

Prepare your favorite sweet short pastry. Line tart tins or foil. For a variety, pipe or drop from a teaspoon approximately 1/2 teaspoon of raspberry, strawberry or apricot jam on the pastry.

Prepare filling; whip together the butter and powdered sugar for 3 minutes - until light and fluffy. Sift the all-purpose and corn flour together and add pinch of salt. Slowly add to butter mixture, blend well and then whip for 2 minutes. The texture should be smooth and light similar to thick frosting.

Blend in 1 teaspoon vanilla and any coloring you may wish to add (pink or yellow). Place mixture in a piping bag with star tube and pipe over the jam on the pastry in a circular motion. Bake at 400° F. for about 15 minutes, cool and dust with powdered sugar. Makes 24 tarts.

TEA NOTE:
Mavis Redman of the British Pantry provided this recipe to us from her father's recipe file. She recommends a pot of Darjeeling or Ceylon blend as the perfect accompaniment.

Nutritional Analysis per Serving
Calories: 231, Total Fat: 15.7 g., Saturated Fat: 9.6 g.
Cholesterol: 41 mg., Carbohydrate: 21.3 g., Dietary Fiber: .7 g.
Protein: 2.0 g., Sodium: 158 mg.

FRESH NECTARINE TART

Ken's youngest daughter Mandy Lewis is a dental hygienist in New Zealand. That doesn't keep her from having a sweet tooth. Here's her recipe.

Crust:
1-1/4	cup flour
1/4	tsp. salt
1/2	cup butter, cut in chunks
2	T. sour cream
4	large ripe nectarines, peeled and thinly sliced.

Custard:
4	T. sour cream
1	cup sugar
1/4	cup flour
1/4	tsp. salt
1/4	tsp. almond extract
1/4	tsp. mace
3	egg yolks

Preheat oven to 375° F.

To make crust, place butter chunks in food processor fitted with steel blade. Pour flour, salt, and 2 tablespoons sour cream over butter and process until mixture is crumbly. Press mixture into bottom of greased 9" tart pan with removable bottom. Bake 20 minutes or until lightly golden. Arrange nectarine slices over crust in concentric circles overlapping slightly for a petal design.

To make the custard, combine remaining sour cream, sugar, flour, salt, almond extract, mace and egg yolks in processor and process 5 to 10 seconds or until blended. Pour over nectarines.

Bake 35 to 40 minutes or until firm. Cool on wire rack. When completely cooled, remove sides of tart pan. Serve at room temperature, but store in refrigerator. 18 Servings

Nutritional Analysis per Serving
Calories: 161, Total Fat: 7.2 g., Saturated Fat: 4.1 g.
Cholesterol: 51 mg., Carbohydrate: 22.9 g., Dietary Fiber: .5 g.
Protein: 2.0 g., Sodium: 115 mg.

TEA TIME SWEETS

JUDITH'S NORWEGIAN RICE PUDDING

Judith's Tearooms and Rose Cafe • Poulsbo, Washington

Judith Goodrich, owner of Judith's Tearooms and Rose Cafe in Poulsbo, has patrons who make the trip to Poulsbo just to have this " light and truly Norwegian pudding."

1-1/2	cups rice
4	cups water
1	tsp. salt

1/2	cup sugar
1	T. cinnamon
1	T. vanilla
2	cups raspberries or lingonberries
1	pint heavy whipping cream
1	T. sugar

Bring water and salt to a boil. Add rice and boil for 10 minutes. Reduce heat and simmer 10 minutes more. Set aside When cooled, gently stir in sugar, cinnamon and vanilla. Refrigerate.

Whip fresh heavy cream with just a little sugar. Set aside. If fresh berries are in season, use them, but if using frozen berries, take as much care as possible to not crush the fruit. Do not add sugar to the berries. The blend of tart and sweet is what makes this a special treat.

Just before assembling, fold the whipped cream into the rice porridge. Using wine glasses, layer the pudding with the berries and continue layering. Top with a dollop of whipped cream. Makes approximately 10 servings.

Nutritional Analysis per Serving
Calories: 324, Total Fat: 18 g., Saturated Fat: 11 g.
Cholesterol: 65 mg., Carbohydrate: 38.3 g., Dietary Fiber: 2.4 g.
Protein: 3.2 g., Sodium: 236 mg.

MARYSVILLE WHITE-CHOCOLATE STRAWBERRIES

1   pint (2 cups) fresh strawberries
6   oz. white chocolate

Wash and pat dry the berries. Leave the hulls on. Melt white chocolate in top of double boiler over hot water (not boiling). Holding strawberries by the stem, dip about 2/3 of each berry into chocolate. Let excess drip off, then set strawberry on a baking sheet. Repeat for all berries, chill for 1/2 hour or until chocolate is solid. Serve chilled. Makes about 12 dipped strawberries.

Nutritional Analysis per Dipped Strawberry
Calories: 116, Total Fat: 5.4 g., Saturated Fat: 2.9 g.
Cholesterol: 0 mg., Carbohydrate: 18.9 g., Dietary Fiber: 4.2 g.
Protein: 1.5 g., Sodium: 4 mg.

ANNIE'S BREAD PUDDING

Annie Fenwick's Tea Room • Gresham, Oregon

"Like the word itself, pudding is quietly unassuming and soothing . . .
[it has] an honesty and dignity all its own."
Jennifer Wilkinson
Traditional Home Magazine

4	cups cubed, buttered bread
2	cups milk, scalded
1/2	cup sugar
2	eggs slightly beaten
1/4	tsp. salt
1	tsp. cinnamon
	Zest of 1 lemon
1	tsp. lemon extract
2	tsp. almond extract
1/2	cup raisins (optional)

Place buttered bread in oven proof dish. Blend remaining ingredients and pour over bread cubes. Place dish in pan of water 1" deep. Bake 40-45 minutes, or until silver knife comes out clean.

Serve warm with "Toriani" butterscotch syrup and whipped cream. Makes 12 servings.

Nutritional Analysis per Serving
Calories: 261, Total Fat: 5.5 g., Saturated Fat: 2.6 g.
Cholesterol: 46 mg., Carbohydrate: 45.8 g., Dietary Fiber: .4 g.
Protein: 7 g., Sodium: 731 mg.

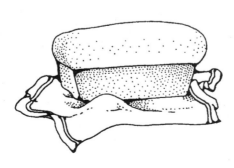

JENNY'S NEW ZEALAND PAVLOVA

Pavlova was a tea treat originally created in Australia at the turn of the century as a tribute to the touring Russian ballerina of that name. This recipe was adapted by Ken's oldest daughter, Jenny Lewis, a teacher in Auckland, New Zealand:

6	egg whites
2	cups extra-fine sugar (available at specialty British markets, but simple to make by processing regular granulated sugar a few seconds in your blender)
1-1/2	tsp. white vinegar
1-1/2	tsp. vanilla
1	T. cornstarch
2	cups whipping cream Fresh fruit in season, kiwis and strawberries are especially nice

In a metal bowl, beat egg whites to stiff peaks. Add one tablespoon sugar at a time until all has been added and the egg whites are glossy (15-20 minutes) Fold in vanilla, vinegar and cornstarch.

Preheat oven to 300° F. Line baking sheet with foil. Butter the foil and outline a 7" circle. Heap the egg mixture onto the circle, molding the sides higher with a slight depression in the center.

Place on bottom rack and bake 45 minutes. Turn off the heat and leave until oven is cool. Meanwhile whip the cream and set aside. Remove the egg meringue from oven and top with the whipped cream and sliced kiwis, strawberries, blueberries, blackberies or any combination of fresh fruit. Serve immediately. Makes 6 servings.

Nutritional Analysis per Serving
Calories: 555, Total Fat: 29.4 g., Saturated Fat: 18.3 g.
Cholesterol: 109 mg., Carbohydrate: 70.6 g., Dietary Fiber: .2 g.
Protein: 5.1 g., Sodium: 85 mg.

APRICOT BAKED PEARS

"What beautiful fruit! I love fruit when it's expensive."
Sir Arthur Wing Pinero
The Second Mrs. Tanqueray

Local pears are good even though they're not expensive, and this is particularly wonderful on a chilly evening.

1/3	cup apricot jam
1/4	cup orange juice
4	medium pears, halved, peeled and cored
	Whipped cream (optional)
	Ground nutmeg (optional)

In a baking dish, stir together the jam and the orange juice. Place pears in dish, cut side down; spoon sauce over top. Bake covered, at 350° F. for 25 to 30 minutes (or until tender).

Serve warm in individual dessert dish. Spoon sauce over pears. If desired, top with whipped cream and sprinkle with nutmeg. Makes 4 servings.

Nutritional Analysis per Serving
Calories: 218, Total Fat: 6 g., Saturated Fat: 3.3 g.
Cholesterol: 19 mg., Carbohydrate: 44.3 g., Dietary Fiber: 4.3 g.
Protein: 1.2 g., Sodium: 16 mg.

KIKO'S GREEN TEA ICE CREAM

The green tea flavor is very refreshing. This easy dessert ice cream does not require an ice cream freezer to prepare.

1	qt. heavy cream
1	pint milk
1-1/2	cup sugar
1	heaping tsp. Mattcha (or grind any good green tea into a powder)

Mix the cream, sugar and milk in a large bowl until the sugar dissolves. Place the dry green tea in a measuring cup and add enough warm water to measure 3/4 cup. Mix the tea and water into a thin paste. Add this to the cream, milk, and sugar mixture. Place in the freezer until the mixture is frozen about an inch from the sides all around and slushy in the center. Scoop into blender and blend until smooth, about 2 minutes. Return it to the freezer until completely frozen. Makes 12 servings.

Nutritional Analysis per Serving
Calories: 317, Total Fat: 21.3 g., Saturated Fat: 13.2 g.
Cholesterol: 75 mg., Carbohydrate: 29.9 g., Dietary Fiber: 0.0 g.
Protein: 3.3 g., Sodium: 51 mg.

SWEET SPICED PECANS

I think when "visions of sugarplums danced in their heads" these festive Sweet Spiced Pecans were doing the Macarena too.

1	cup sugar
1-1/2	T. ground cinnamon
1	tsp. ground cloves
1	tsp. salt
1	tsp. ground ginger
1/2	tsp. ground nutmeg
1	egg white
1	T. cold water
1	pound pecans

Preheat oven to 250° F. Butter a large jelly roll pan.

Mix together thoroughly all dry ingredients. (May be done in food processor.) Beat egg white with cold water until frothy but not stiff. Add spiced sugar mixture and stir well. Add nuts; stir well to coat.

Spread nuts in pan, place in oven and bake for 1 hour, stirring to separate every 15 to 20 minutes. Remove from oven when dry and toasty.

Cool. Store in airtight container. Makes 16 one ounce servings.

Nutritional Analysis per Serving
Calories: 242, Total Fat: 19.3 g., Saturated Fat: 1.6 g.
Cholesterol: 0 mg., Carbohydrate: 18.4 g., Dietary Fiber: 2.6 g.
Protein: 2.5 g., Sodium: 138 mg.

GRAND MARNIER
CHOCOLATE TRUFFLES

Ken grew up in Liverpool, England, where every dessert is referred to as "pudding" and still ends a meal with the hopeful query "What's for puddin', luv?" These are far better than puddin' . . .

8 oz. plain, but high quality,
milk chocolate bar (we like Cadbury's)
2 -3 T. whipping cream
2 T. Grand Marnier liqueur
1 egg, slightly beaten
3/4 tsp. grated orange rind
2 T. unsalted butter

Coatings: cocoa, finely chopped nuts, chocolate sprinkles, or coconut

Melt chocolate over low heat in double boiler. Warm up the whipping cream and stir it into the chocolate. Remove from heat and immediately add the liqueur. Whisk in egg, orange rind and butter until the mixture is smooth. Refrigerate for 2 hours, until it is firm. Using a melon scoop or teaspoon, scoop out chocolate and roll into balls. Roll in the coating you choose. Refrigerate immediately, or freeze. Makes about 2 dozen truffles.

Nutritional Analysis per Serving
Calories: 75, Total Fat: 5.1 g., Saturated Fat: 2.8 g.
Cholesterol: 15 mg., Carbohydrate: 6.3 g., Dietary Fiber: .4 g.
Protein: 1.2 g., Sodium: 11 mg.

THE CONNAUGHT HOTEL'S TRIFLE

*Conceived as a London residence for the landed gentry, this dignified
hotel was built in 1897 and named in honor
of Queen Victoria's third son.*

Sponge:	5	eggs.
	2/3	cup sugar.
	1	cup all-purpose flour.

Syrup:	3	T. water.
	3	T.sugar.
	3	T. dry sherry
	1	T. rum

Custard:	2	egg yolks.
	1	egg.
	1/4	cup sugar.
	1	T. cornstarch.
	1-1/2	cup milk
	1	cup black currant or cherry jelly.

Whipped Cream:	1	cup whipping cream.
	1	T. sugar.
	1	T. sifted sugar powder.
	1	T. vanilla.
	1	cup fresh raspberries.
	1/4	cup toasted sliced almonds.
	1/4	cup chopped pistachio nuts.

For sponge cake; Grease and lightly flour a 9x9x2 inch
baking pan.

In a large mixing bowl, beat the 5 eggs with an electric
mixer on high speed for about 4 minutes or until thick.
Gradually add the 2/3 cup of sugar; beat at medium
speed for 4-5 minutes or until light and fluffy. Fold in the
flour. Turn batter into prepared pan. Bake in a 350° F.
oven for 20 minutes or until top springs pack when
touched lightly. Remove and cool in pan on a wire rack
for 10 minutes. Remove from pan and cool completely.

Meanwhile, for syrup; Place 3 tablespoons water and 3 tablespoons sugar in a small saucepan. Bring to boil, remove from heat, stir in the sherry and rum. Cool to room temperature.

For custard; Beat together the yolks and one egg, set aside. In a medium saucepan stir together the1/4 cup sugar and the cornstarch. Stir in milk. Cook and stir over medium heat until thickened and bubbly. Cook and stir for 2 minutes more. Remove from heat. Gradually stir about half of the hot mixture into the beaten egg mixture. Return all of the egg mixture to the saucepan. Cook and stir until nearly bubbly, but do not boil. Reduce heat, cook and stir 2 minutes more. Remove from heat and cool slightly.

When cake is cool, split in half horizontally. Spread the cut side of the bottom layer with the jelly. Replace the top layer of the cake. Cut the cake into 3/4-inch cubes. Place the cake cubes in a 2- 3 quart glass bowl. Pour the cooled syrup over the cake cubes. Pour warm custard over all. Cover and chill.

Just before serving, place the whipping cream, one table-spoon sugar, powdered sugar, and vanilla in a medium mixing bowl.

Beat with an electric mixer until stiff peaks form, smooth over top of trifle and garnish with the almonds and pisachio nuts topping them with the fresh raspberries and sprigs of mint. Yields about 24 servings.

Nutritional Analysis per Serving
Calories: 182, Total Fat: 7.4 g., Saturated Fat: 3.3 g.
Cholesterol: 87 mg., Carbohydrate: 25.8 g:, Dietary Fiber: .8 g.
Protein: 3.7 g., Sodium: 33 mg.

THEME TEAS

All too often, those of us who did not grow up with Afternoon Tea develop some misconceptions about it. Fostered by Masterpiece Theater and fueled by supermarket gothic romance novels, an Afternoon Tea could indeed be envisioned as intimidating with an oh-so-proper protocol and stodgy ritual altogether alien to our Northwest lifestyle. But as you will learn firsthand by visiting the tearooms in this book, tea simply is not stiff, uncomfortable, or rigidly formal at all.

Teas can be the perfect backdrop for any festive event, whether it be the return of the hummingbirds in spring or a bridal shower, a child's birthday or announcing an engagement, teas are always appropriate and fun. In an era where alcohol has fallen from favor, a tea setting can even provide a millenium alternative to cocktail parties that is healthy, sane and civil.

We have presented some of our favorite theme teas throughout the book (see the index under "theme teas"). Additionally, we would like to offer the following list of events and excuses to gather friends and loved ones to enjoy some taste treats and a good cuppa. Cheers!

MORE IDEAS FOR THEME TEAS

Children's Teas:

Teddy Bear Tea

Mad Hatter's Tea

Easter Bunny Tea

Fourth of July Tea

Four-Legged Friend Tea

Gingerbread Tea

Grown-Up Teas:

Valentine's Day Tea

St. Patrick's Day Tea

Graduation Tea

Bridal Tea

Baby Shower Tea

Harvest Tea

Angel Tea

SPREADS &
CONDIMENTS

Apple Ginger Chutney

*When my grandparents lived on the cold plains of Alberta,
my grandmother longed to live somewhere that she could grow apple
trees. She found that place in subsequent homes in British Columbia
and Washington, and here is her tangy chutney.*

4	large Granny Smith apples, peeled, cored, and chopped
2	cups minced onion
1-1/2	cups cider vinegar
1-1/2	cups firmly packed brown sugar
1	cup golden raisins
1/4	cup minced peeled fresh ginger root
1	red bell pepper, minced
3/4	tsp. dry mustard
3/4	tsp. salt
1/2	tsp. dried hot red pepper flakes

In large saucepan combine the apples, onion, vinegar,
brown sugar, raisins, ginger root, bell pepper, mustard,
salt, and the red pepper flakes. Bring the mixture to a
boil, stirring, and cook over moderate heat, stirring occasionally for 40 minutes, or until it has thickened. Spoon
into glass jars with tight-fitting lids or seal in freezer bags.
This chutney keeps, covered and chilled, for 2 weeks.
Makes about 6 cups (24 - 2 oz. servings).

*Nutritional Analysis per Serving
Calories: 69, Total Fat: .1 g., Saturated Fat: 0 g.
Cholesterol: 0 mg., Carbohydrate: 18.1 g., Dietary Fiber: .9 g.
Protein: .4 g., Sodium: 121 mg.*

AUNT MARWAYNE'S PLUM CHUTNEY

*"Try this chutney spread thinly on a tea sandwich of turkey or chicken,
with a little bit of mayonnaise,"* says my aunt, the astrologer,
Marwayne Leipzig.

8	cups (pitted, cut up) ripe blue Italian plums
2	cups raisins
1	cup brown sugar
1	cup onion, chopped
1/2	cup vinegar
10	cloves of garlic, minced
8	T. mustard seed
2	T. chopped ginger
1/2	tsp. cayenne pepper

In a pot over medium-low heat, cook all the ingredients
for about an hour.

Freeze in small freezer-safe containers, or spoon into hot
jelly jars and seal the same way you would when putting
up jam or jelly. Yields about 60 servings

Nutritional Analysis per Serving
Calories: 44, Total Fat: .6 g., Saturated Fat: 0 g.
Cholesterol: 0 mg., Carbohydrate: 10 g., Dietary Fiber: .7 g.
Protein: .8 g., Sodium: 12 mg.

CALICO CREAM CHEESE

Pomeroy House • Yacolt, Washington

A colorful, fresh tasting sandwich spread.

Combine in a medium bowl;

8	oz. cream cheese softened
1/4	green pepper chopped into 1/4" cubes
1/4	yellow or orange pepper chopped into 1/4" cubes
1/4	red pepper chopped into 1/4" cubes
1	T grated onion
1/4	tsp. anchovy paste
	salt and pepper to taste

Generously spead filling on party rye bread and garnish with fresh dill sprigs.

Nutritional Analysis per two-tablespoon serving
Calories: 51, Total Fat: 5 g., Saturated Fat: 3.1 g.
Cholesterol: 16 mg., Carbohydrate: .7 g., Dietary Fiber: .1 g.
Protein: 1.1 g., Sodium: 78 mg.

QUEEN MARY'S LEMON CURD

Queen Mary • Seattle, Washington

This recipe is from England where it has graced the Greengo family tea tables for at least four generations. It's now a favorite with patrons of Queen Mary.

10	egg yolks
13	oz. fresh lemon juice
1/2	teaspoon salt
1	packet of gelatin
1	lb., 2 oz. granulated sugar
1/2	lb. butter
	peel of 4 lemons

Combine egg yolks, sugar and lemon juice in heavy-bottom saucepan and stir until almost boiling. Over medium heat whisk in the rest of the ingredients.

Bloom gelatin in cold water, dissolve over low heat and add to hot mixture, stir to incorporate. Strain.

Yields about 40 servings.

TEA NOTE:
The suggested tea to complement is Earl Grey or Queen Victoria blend.

Nutritional Analysis per Serving
Calories: 108, Total Fat: 5.9 g., Saturated Fat: 3.3 g.
Cholesterol: 66 mg., Carbohydrate: 14.2 g., Dietary Fiber: .3 g.
Protein: .9 g., Sodium: 76 mg.

LOW FAT CREAMY PEACH SPREAD

(for fat-free crumpets or muffins)

Shelley's Spot of Tea • Tacoma, Washington

1/2   half fresh peach
1   cup peach yogurt
1/2   cup Light Cool Whip

Cut peach into very small pieces (do not use blender). Whip yogurt and Cool Whip together and blend in the peaches. Serve as a side dish on the tea tray. About 12 servings.

(Can be frozen.)

Nutritional Analysis per Serving
Calories: 26, Total Fat: .2 g., Saturated Fat: .1 g.
Cholesterol: 1 mg., Carbohydrate: 4.6 g., Dietary Fiber: .1 g.
Protein: .8 g., Sodium: 13 mg.

BEVERAGES

LEMONADE COOLER

Village Tea Room • Edmonds, Washington

8 tea bags
3 quarts boiling water
3/4 cup sugar
1 (12 oz.) can lemonade
Lemon slices
Mint
1 (32 oz.) bottle ginger ale, chilled

Place tea bags in boiling water and steep 10 minutes. remove tea bags. Add sugar and stir until desolved. Add lemonade and chill.

Just before serving add ginger ale. Garnish with mint sprig. Yield 16 cups.

ICED REPUBLIC CHAI

Plaza Escada • Vancouver, B.C.

8 tsp. of Republic of Chai, (available wherever Republic of Tea line is sold)
6 cups boiling water.
2 orange slices
1 T. white sugar or honey
2 cups of milk

Pour boiling water over chai and steep 4 to 5 minutes. Strain tea into pitcher containing orange slices and sugar or honey. Allow to cool completely.

Remove orange slices. Add milk to tea mixture. Garnish with fresh orange slices and cinnamon sticks.

ENJOY!

APPENDIX

TeaTime in the Northwest

Glossary of Tea Terms

Agony of the leaves - Tea tasters expression descriptive of the unfolding of the leaves when boiling water is applied.

Assam - High grade tea grown in Assam Province in Northeast India.

Aroma - Denotes that both the tea leaf and infusion have one of a certain number of smells which are highly valued. Such aroma is connected with flavor and is highly fragrant.

Autumnal teas - Term applied to India and Formosa teas, meaning teas touched with cool weather.

Biscuity - A pleasant aroma associated with a well-fired Assam

Black tea - Any tea that has been thoroughly fermented before being fired as opposed to green or Oolong tea.

Blend - A mixture of different growths.

Body - A liquor having both fullness and strength as opposed to a thin liquor.

Bright - Sparkling red liquor. Denotes good tea which has life as opposed to a dull looking infused leaf or liquor.

Brisk - "live" not flat liquor. Usually of pungent character.

Caffeine content - In a cup of tea, less than 1 grain; in a cup of coffee, 1.5 grain.

Ch'a - (Char)(Chai) Chinese. Tea.

Color - Color of liquor which varies from country to country and district to district.

Darjeeling - The finest and most delicately flavored of the Indian teas. Grown chiefly in the Himalayan Mountains at elevations ranging from 2,500 to 6,500 feet.

Even - Tea leaf which is true to grade and consisting of pieces of roughly equal size. When applied to infused leaf it is usually combined with bright and coppery.

Fermented (black) tea - Chinese refer to black tea as "hong Cha" or "Red tea" because when it is brewed it takes on a reddish-orange color. More popular often among Westerners than Chinese. Often used to make specialty blends with the addition of Jasmine blossoms or spices.

Full - Strong tea, without bitterness, having color and substanceas opposed to thin and empty.

Garden - Used intrchangeably with "plantation" in some tea countries, but usually referrind to an estate unit.

Garden mark - The mark put on tea chests by the estate to identify its particular product.

Goddess - A semi fermented tea. Has a stern taste and is credited as an aid to digestion.

Green tea - Tea leaves that have been sterilized either in live steam, hot air, or hot pans, whereby fermentation is prevented, and then rolled and dried.

Handkerchief tea - From the island of Formosa. It gets its name from the fact that Chinese tea growers bring down from their little gardens or farms verry tippy teas, often of the highest quality, in large silk handkerchiefs.

Ichiban-Cha - Japanese for "first tea," or first plucking.

Malty - Slightly high-fired tea, like Keemun

Mature - No flatness or rawness.

Monster - Dutch for "sample."

Nose - The aroma of tea.

Oolong - From the Chinese wu-lung meaning "black dragon." A semi femented tea of fine quality, hand rolled and fired in baskets over pits containing red-hot charcoal. Originally shipped principally from Guanzhou and Amoy in China, the production of Oolong was introduced more than a century ago to Taiwan.

Sappy - Full juicy liquor.

Scented tea - Made in China and Taiwan by introducing jasmine, gardenia, or yulan blossoms during the firing and packing process.

Self drinking - Tasting of smoke, used interchangeably with the term "tarry."

Smoky - In tea tasting, a tea is said to "stand-up" when it holds its original color and flavor.

Standing up - In tea tasting, a tea is said to "stand-up" when it holds its original color and flavor.

Stand out - Liquor above the average.

Stewy - Soft liquor, lacking point.

Strength - Thick liquor, pungent and brisk.

Sweet - A light, not undesirable liquor.

TeaTime in the Northwest

Tea - Tea is the tender leaves, leaf, buds, and tender internodes of different varieties of Thea sinesis prepared and cured by recognized methods of manufacture.

Tip - The bud leaf of the tea plant.

Tippy tea - Teas with white or golden tips. (See handkerchief tea.)

Well twisted - Leaf which is tightly rolled or twisted which is indicative of ideally withered tea.

TEA SUPPLIERS

Backroads Fine Teas
P.O. Box 1019
Hayward, WI 54843

Barnes & Watson Fine Teas
1319 Dexter Avenue N. #30
Seattle, WA 98109

Blue Willow Tea
911 E. Pike
Seattle, WA 98122

The British Gourmet
45 Wall St.
Madison, CT 06443

C.B.I. / Xanadu Teas
2181 N.W. Nicolai St.
Portland, OR 97210

Camellia Tea Company
P.O. Box 8310
Metairie, LA 70011-8310

Celestial Seasonings
4600 Sleepytime Dr.
Boulder, CO 80301

Choice Organic Teas
2901 N.E. Blakely
Seattle, WA 98105

Christopher Reeves Brookes Co
10752 Bill Point Dr
Bainbridge Island, WA 98110

O.H. Clapp & Co.
42 Riverside Avenue
Westport, CT 06880

Crabtree & Evelyn, Ltd.
Box 167
Woodstock Hill, CT 06284

East India Tea
1481 - Third St.
San Francisco, CA 94107

East Indies Co.
7 Keystone Dr.
Lebanon, PA 17042

Eastern Shore Tea
550 Main St.
Church Hill, MD 21623

Eden Tea
701 Tecumseh Road
Clinton, MI 49236

Eterni Tea
963 Utsalady Road
Camano Island, WA 98292

First Colony Tea
204-222 West 22nd St.
P.O. Box 11005
Norfolk, VA 23517

Fortnum & Mason Ltd.
Piccadilly, London
England W1A 1ER

Fox Mountian Farm
1600 Chippewa St.
New Orleans, LA 70130

Golden Moon Tea
P.O. Box 1646
Woodinville, WA 98072

Grace Tea Company
50 W. 17th
New York, NY 10011

Harney & Sons Fine Teas
P.O. Box 638
Salisbury, CT 06068

Lindsay's Teas
380 Swift Ave. Suite 10
South San Francisco, CA 94080

Continued on next page

TEA SUPPLIERS

Market Spice Tea
85-A Pike Place
Seattle, WA 98101

McNulty's
109 Christopher St.
New York, NY 10014

Paprika Weiss Importers
1546 Second Avenue
New York, NY 10028

Peet's Coffee, Tea, & Spice
2124 Vine St.
Berkeley, CA 94708

The Republic of Tea
8 Digital Dr. Suite 100
Novato, CA 94949

M. Rohrs
1692 Second Avenue
New York, NY 10028

Rose Tree Cottage
824 E. California Blvd.
Pasadena, CA 91106

Royal Gardens Tea
P.O. Box 2390
Fort Bragg, CA 95437

Schapira's Coffee & Tea
Box 327 Factory Lane
Pine Plains, NY 12567

Simpson and Vail
53 Park Place
New York, NY 10007

Stash Tea
P.O. Box 910
Portland, OR 97207

Tazo Teas
P.O. Box 66
Portland, OR 97207

Tea Association of the USA *
Tea Council of the USA
230 Park Avenue
New York, NY 10169

The Tea Club
1715 N. Burling St.
Chicago, IL 60614

Tea to You
3712 N. Broadway/Box 471
Chicago, IL 60613

Tea Planters &
Importers Company
55/56 Aldgate High Street
London, England

Todd & Holland Tea Merchants
417 Lathrop Avenue
River Forest, IL 60305

Water and Leaves
380 Swift Ave. #6
So. San Francisco, CA 94080

Yogi Tea
8401 Santa Monica Blvd
W. Hollywood, CA 90069

Many of the tea rooms listed in this book are also excellent sources for teas and teatime accessories.

* Supply tea information only

Index

Index

Index

Index

<u>Lisa's</u> - lovely, tasteful, very large but divided rooms gives feeling of privacy. Overpriced except for tea - nice choice. Enjoyed apricot tea. Entrees were fair - very small portions* Excellent selection of gifts - good prices. Empty on Sat. nite. Spoke w/ owner (John) - very helpful... used to be franchise but Lisa got out of business. still supplies her tea blends. Bought cute notepads (2.98 ea.)

* creative menu sounds better than is.

<u>Sorrento's</u> - classic hotel ambiance - lovely service in lobby lounge on tiered servers - nice choice of mini treats - passion tea very good. Marred by "smoking" in room! Taped music too soft to hear... mix of cocktails/lounge not good w/ tea atmosphere. Cozy fireplace - price appropriate.

<u>Teacup</u> - great fun tasting & sniffing tea blends. Bought "La Belle Helene" + "Old Man's Tea". Nice gift choices - bought teapot earrings + child's cookbook - linen towel - all good prices. Very limited sweets. Counter space cramped... but friendly.

TeaTime
in the Northwest

Report Form

Tea is quietly blossoming in the Northwest with many new tearooms opening each month. If you discover a new tea room, or know of an old favorite that was not included in *TeaTime in the Northwest*, please take a minute to let us know so that future editions will reflect the growth and diversity of the region's tea culture. If you have comments about any of the tea rooms listed in *TeaTime in the Northwest*, we would be interested in your experiences and opinions.

Name of new tea room or establishment

_____

Address _____

_____

Phone _____

Comments _____

_____

_____

Comments about tea rooms listed in TeaTime in the Northwest

_____

_____

_____

Signed _____

Your Name and Address _____

_____

Thank you for your input!

Please send to: Sharon & Ken Foster-Lewis
298 W. Parkside Dr.
Camano Island, WA 98292

TeaTime in the Northwest